PENGUIN MODERN MASTERS

NOAM CHOMSKY

Born in England in 1932, John Lyons was edu-
cated at St. Bede's College, Manchester, and at
Cambridge, where he received his bachelor's
degree in 1953. He served in the Royal Navy as
an interpreter of Russian from 1954 to 1956, then
returned to Cambridge to earn his master's and
doctoral degrees and to lecture in linguistics from
1961 to 1964. He has taught in the United States
at Indiana University, UCLA, and the University
of Illinois and is currently Professor of Linguistics at the University of Sussex. In addition to
the present volume, he is the author of *Structural
Semantics* and *Introduction to Theoretical Linguistics*.

Frank Kermode, King Edward VII Professor of
English Literature at Cambridge, is the author of
The Classic; *D.H. Lawrence*; *Shakespeare, Spen-
ser, Donne*; and other widely acclaimed critical
studies.

MODERN MASTERS

ALREADY PUBLISHED

PENGUIN
MODERN MASTERS

EDITED BY frank kermode

By Modern Masters we mean the men who have changed and are changing the life and thought of our age. The authors of these volumes are themselves masters, and they have written their books in the belief that general discussion of their subjects will henceforth be more informed and more exciting than ever before. —**F. K.**

noam
chomsky

Revised Edition

john lyons

PENGUIN BOOKS

Penguin Books Ltd, Harmondsworth,
Middlesex, England
Penguin Books, 40 West 23rd Street,
New York, New York 10010, U.S.A.
Penguin Books Australia Ltd, Ringwood,
Victoria, Australia
Penguin Books Canada Limited, 2801 John Street,
Markham, Ontario, Canada L3R 1B4
Penguin Books (N.Z.) Ltd, 182–190 Wairau Road,
Auckland 10, New Zealand

First published in Great Britain by William Collins 1970
First published in the United States of America by
The Viking Press 1970
Reprinted 1971 (3 times), 1972, 1973, 1974, 1976
Published in Penguin Books in a revised edition 1978
Reprinted 1979, 1981, 1984

LIBRARY OF CONGRESS CATALOGING IN PUBLICATION DATA
Lyons, John.
Noam Chomsky.
(Penguin modern masters)
Bibliography: p. 183
Includes index.
1. Chomsky, Noam.   2. Linguists—
United States—Biography.
[P85.C47L9 1978]   410.92'4 [B]   77–21346
ISBN 0 14 00.4370 5

Printed in the United States of America by
Kingsport Press, Inc., Kingsport, Tennessee
Set in Linotype Primer

PREFACE
TO THE FIRST EDITION

I should like to record here my gratitude to Noam Chomsky for reading and commenting upon the manuscript of this book. The fact that it has been read in advance by Chomsky (and corrected in a number of places) encourages me in the belief that it gives a reasonably fair and reliable account of his views on linguistics and the philosophy of language. There are of course a number of points, especially in the final chapter, where Chomsky is not in entire agreement with what I have to say. But these points of disagreement will be obvious enough either from the text itself or from the footnotes that I have added.

My main purpose in writing the book has been to provide the reader with enough of the historical and technical background for him to go on afterward to Chomsky's own works. I am aware that certain sections of my book are fairly demanding. But I do not believe that it is possible to understand even Chomsky's less technical works or to appreciate the impact his ideas are having in a number of different disciplines without going into some of the details of the formal system for the description of language that he has constructed.

J. C. Marshall and P. H. Matthews have also been kind enough to read the book for me in manuscript, and I have made many changes in the final version as a result of their comments. I am deeply indebted to them for their assistance. Needless to say, I am myself solely responsible for any errors or imperfections that still remain in the text.

Edinburgh
October 1969

J.L.

PREFACE
TO THE REVISED EDITION

In preparing this revised and enlarged edition I have left the first seven chapters almost unchanged (except for the correction of some misprints and minor errors). However, I have brought the Introduction up to date by adding a little material and changing a few phrases, and I have inserted one or two footnotes drawing the reader's attention to the appendixes. Chapter viii, on developments that have been taking place in the field of generative grammar since the late 1960s, is wholly new; and fairly extensive additions have been made to what are now chapters ix–xi.

Somewhat to my surprise, the book has been widely used by students (for whom it was not primarily intended). This being so, I thought that it might be helpful if I included, as an appendix, a semiformal account of the formalism upon which Chomsky's system of generative grammar rests and, no less important, some cautionary comments about the complexity of the relationship between generative grammars and natural languages. Mathematically minded readers will forgive me, I trust, if I have not gone into the formalism, even in this appendix, as fully as they might have liked. If their appetite is whetted but not satisfied, they will find references to Chomsky's own more technical work in the suggestions for further reading that I have appended to the expanded and updated Bibliography.

The second short Appendix is intended to correct what many have taken to be a certain imbalance, not to say prejudice, in my presentation of Chomsky as a "modern master." On the whole, I stand by my own assessment of the significance of Chomsky's work; but I now see, in the light of what Chomsky himself says in the recently published version of *The Logical Structure of Linguistic Theory* (to which I draw attention in Appendix 2), that there may have been less difference than I thought (on the basis of his published work) between Chomsky's earlier and later views. I have also thought it appropriate that I should respond, in Appendix 2, however briefly, to some of the criticisms that Dell Hymes made in his gratifyingly lengthy and careful review of the first edition and that, in doing so, I should acknowledge my indebtedness to a scholar whose knowledge of the subject is in many respects greater than my own and who, for reasons best known to himself, considered my unambitious little book worthy of detailed comment. I have learned a great deal from his review, even where I disagree with the points that are made; and I recommend it to everyone for the background information that it contains about American linguistics and American academic life and attitudes in the 1960s, when Chomsky emerged as a political thinker and activist. I have, admittedly and by design, said relatively little about this in my book. It would have been an impertinence for a non-American to have attempted to; and, in my view at least, important though Chomsky's political ideas are in any portrayal of him as a man, it is his theory of language that makes him a "master of modern thought."

Sussex
March 1977

J.L.

CONTENTS

BIOGRAPHICAL NOTE

Avram Noam Chomsky was born in Philadelphia, Pennsylvania, on December 7, 1928. He received his early education at the Oak Lane Country Day School and the Central High School, Philadelphia, and then went on to the University of Pennsylvania, where he studied linguistics, mathematics, and philosophy. It was at the University of Pennsylvania that he took his Ph.D., although most of the research that led to this degree was carried out as a Junior Fellow of the Society of Fellows at Harvard University between 1951 and 1955. Since 1955 he has taught at the Massachusetts Institute of Technology, where he now holds the Ferrari P. Ward Chair of Modern Languages and Linguistics. He is married, with two daughters and a son.

Chomsky's work has been widely acclaimed in academic circles. He has been awarded several honorary doctorates: by the University of Chicago (1967), the University of London (1967), Loyola University (1970), Swarthmore College (1970), Bard College (1971), the

University of Delhi (1972), the University of Massachusetts (1973). He is a Fellow of the American Society for the Advancement of Science; a member of the National Academy of Sciences, the American Academy of Arts and Sciences, and the American Academy of Political and Social Sciences; and a Corresponding Fellow of the British Academy. He has been a Visiting Fellow at Columbia University (1957–58), a Fellow of the Institute of Advanced Studies at Princeton University (1958–59), the Linguistic Society of America Professor at the University of California at Los Angeles (1966), the Beckman Professor at the University of California at Berkeley (1966–67). He has delivered the John Locke Lectures at Oxford University (1969), the Shearman Memorial Lectures at the University of London (1969), the Trinity College Bertrand Russell Memorial Lectures at Cambridge University (1971).

Chomsky first made his reputation in linguistics. He had learned something of the principles of historical linguistics from his father, who was a Hebrew scholar of considerable repute. (Chomsky himself did some of his earliest linguistic research, for the degree of M.A., on modern spoken Hebrew.) But the work for which he is now famous, the construction of a system of generative grammar, developed out of his interest in modern logic and the foundations of mathematics, and was only subsequently applied to the description of natural languages. Of considerable importance in Chomsky's intellectual development was the influence of Zellig Harris, Professor of Linguistics at the University of Pennsylvania; and Chomsky himself has explained that it was really his sympathy with Harris's political views that led him to work as an undergraduate in linguistics. There is a sense, therefore, in which politics brought him into linguistics.

Chomsky has been interested in politics since childhood. His views were formed in what he refers to as "the radical Jewish community in New York" and have always tended toward socialism or anarchism. In the 1960s he became one of the leading critics of American foreign policy; and his book of essays on this topic, *American Power and the New Mandarins,* is widely recognized as one of the most powerful indictments of American involvement in Vietnam to have been published on the subject. It has been followed by several other books on political issues: *For Reasons of State, At War with Asia,* and *Peace in the Middle East?*

NOAM CHOMSKY

Introduction

i

Chomsky's position not only is unique within linguistics at the present time, but is probably unprecedented in the whole history of the subject. His first book, published in 1957, short and relatively nontechnical though it was, revolutionized the scientific study of language, and for many years now he has been speaking with unrivaled authority on all aspects of grammatical theory. This is not to say, of course, that all linguists, or even the majority of them, have accepted the theory of transformational grammar that Chomsky put forward some thirteen years ago in *Syntactic Structures*. They have not. There are at least as many recognizably different "schools" of linguistics throughout the world as there were before the "Chomskyan revolution." But the "transformationalist," or "Chomskyan," school is not just one among many. Right or wrong, Chomsky's theory of grammar is undoubtedly the most dynamic and influential, and no linguist who wishes to keep abreast of current developments in his subject can afford to ignore Chomsky's theoretical pronouncements. Every other "school" of linguistics at the present time tends to define its position in relation to Chomsky's views on particular issues.

However, it is not so much Chomsky's status and reputation among linguists that have made him a "master of modern thought." After all, theoretical linguistics is a rather esoteric subject, which few people had even heard of and still fewer knew anything about until very recently. If it is now more widely recognized as a branch of science that is worthwhile pursuing, not only for its own sake but also for the contributions it can make to other disciplines, this is very largely due to Chomsky. More than a thousand university students and teachers are said to have attended his lectures on the philosophy of language and mind at Oxford University in the spring of 1969. Few of these could have had any previous contact with linguistics, but all of them presumably were convinced, or prepared to be convinced, that it was worth making the intellectual effort required to follow Chomsky's at times quite technical argument; and the lectures were widely reported in the press.

Readers who are not already familiar with Chomsky's work may well be wondering at this point what possible connection there might be between a field of study as specialized as transformational grammar and such better-known and obviously important disciplines as psychology and philosophy. This is a question we shall be discussing in some detail in the later chapters of this book. But it may be worthwhile attempting a more general answer here.

It has often been suggested that man is most clearly distinguished from other animal species, not by the faculty of thought or intelligence, as the standard zoological label *Homo sapiens* might indicate, but by his capacity for language. Indeed, philosophers and psychologists have long debated whether thought in the proper sense of the term is conceivable except as "embodied" in speech or writing. Whether or not this is so, it is obvious that language is of vital importance in every aspect of human activity and that, without language, all but the most rudimentary kind of communication would be impossible. Granted that language is essential to human life as we know it, it is only natural to ask what contribution the study of language can make to our understanding of human nature.

But what is language? This is a question that few people even think of asking. In one sense, of course, we all know what we mean by "language"; and our use of the word in everyday conversation depends upon the fact that we all interpret it, as we interpret the other words we use, in the same or in a very similar way. There is, however, a difference between this kind of unreflecting and practical knowledge of what language is and the deeper or more systematic understanding that we should want to call "scientific." As we shall see in the following chapters, it is the aim of theoretical linguistics to give a scientific answer to the question "What is language?" and, in doing so, to provide evidence that philosophers and psychologists can draw upon in their discussion of the relationship that holds between language and thought.

Chomsky's system of transformational grammar was developed, as we shall see, in order to give a mathematically precise description of some of the most striking features of language. Of particular importance in this connection is the ability that children have to derive the structural regularities of their native language—its grammatical rules—from the utterances of their parents and others around them, and then to make use of the same regularities in the construction of utterances they have never heard before. Chomsky has argued, in several of his publications, that the general principles that determine the form of grammatical rules in particular languages, such as English, Turkish, or Chinese, are to some considerable degree common to all human languages. Furthermore, he has claimed that the principles underlying the structure of language are so specific and so highly articulated that they must be regarded as being biologically determined; that is to say, as constituting part of what we call "human nature" and as being genetically transmitted from parents to their children. If this is so, and if it is also the case, as Chomsky maintains, that transformational grammar is the best theory so far developed for the systematic description and explanation of the structure of human language, it is clear that an understanding of transformational grammar is essential for any philosopher, psychologist, or biologist who wishes to take account of man's capacity for language.

The significance of Chomsky's work for disciplines other than linguistics derives primarily, then, from the acknowledged importance of language in all areas of human activity and from the peculiarly intimate relationship that is said to hold between the structure of language and the innate properties or operations of the mind. But language is not the only kind of complex "behavior" that human beings engage in, and there is at least a possibility that other forms of typically human activity (including, perhaps, certain aspects of what we call "artistic creation") will also prove amenable to description within the framework of specially constructed mathematical systems analogous to, or even based upon, transformational grammar. There are many scholars working now in the social sciences and the humanities who believe that this is so. For them, Chomsky's formalization of grammatical theory serves as a model and a standard.

From what has been said in the last few paragraphs it will be clear that Chomsky's influence is now being felt in many different disciplines. So far, however, it is the study of language that has been most profoundly affected by the "Chomskyan revolution," and it is from current research on the grammatical structure of English and other languages that Chomsky draws most of his more general philosophical and psychological views. It is for this reason that we shall give so much attention in the present volume to the linguistic background of Chomsky's thought.

Chomsky's current fame and popularity are not due solely, or even mainly, to his work in linguistics and the effect that this is having on other disciplines. In the 1960's he became widely known as one of the most outspoken and articulate critics of American politics in Vietnam—a "hero of the New Left"—who risked imprisonment by refusing to pay half his taxes and gave support and encouragement to young men refusing to undertake military service in Vietnam. It was undoubtedly for his political writings and his political activity that Chomsky first became famous, especially in the United States—for his condemnation of American "imperialism" and for those academic advisers to the American government who, posing as "experts" in a field where there is no such thing as scientific expertise and where considerations of common morality should have prevailed, have been guilty of deceiving the public about the character of the war in Vietnam, American involvement in Cuba, and other issues. Chomsky's political writings (*American Power and the New Mandarins* and, more recently, *For Reasons of State, The Backroom Boys, At War with Asia, Peace in the Middle East?*) continue to attract attention, and he is still an active supporter of radical social change in the United States.

Although this book is mainly about Chomsky's views on language, it should perhaps be emphasized here that his theory of language and his political philosophy are by no means unconnected, as they might appear to be at first sight. As we shall see in the chapters that follow

Chomsky has long been an opponent of at least the more extreme form of behaviorist psychology, "radical behaviorism," according to which all human knowledge and belief, and all the "patterns" of thought and action characteristic of man, can be explained as "habits" built up by a process of "conditioning," lengthier and more complex no doubt in its details, but not qualitatively different from the process by which rats in a psychological laboratory "learn" to obtain food by pressing a bar in the cage in which they are housed. Chomsky's attack on radical behaviorism was first made in a long and well-documented review of B. F. Skinner's *Verbal Behavior* in 1959, in which Chomsky claimed that the behaviorists' impressive panoply of scientific terminology and statistics was no more than camouflage, covering up their inability to account for the fact that language simply is not a set of "habits" and is radically different from animal communication. It is the same charge that Chomsky has made in his political writings against the sociologists, psychologists, and other social scientists whose "expert" advice is sought by governments: that they "desperately attempt . . . to imitate the surface features of sciences that really have significant intellectual content," neglecting in this attempt all the fundamental problems with which they should be concerned and taking refuge in pragmatic and methodological trivialities. It is Chomsky's conviction that human beings are different from animals or machines and that this difference should be respected both in science and in government, and it is this conviction that underlies and unifies his politics, his linguistics, and his philosophy.

Chomsky's message is familiar enough, and it will find an immediate response in all those who subscribe to a belief in the brotherhood of man and the dignity of human life. Only too often, however, the defense of these traditional values is left to scholars who by academic training are unfitted for the kind of argument that appeals to hardheaded "pragmatists." Chomsky cannot be written off quite so easily as a "woolly-minded liberal." He is as well read in the philosophy of science as his opponents are, and he can manipulate the conceptual and mathematical apparatus of the social sciences with equal ease. His arguments may be accepted or rejected; they cannot be ignored. And anyone who wishes to follow and evaluate these arguments must be prepared to meet Chomsky on his home ground: linguistics, or the scientific investigation of language. For Chomsky believes, as I said earlier, that the structure of language is determined by the structure of the human mind and that the universality of certain properties characteristic of language is evidence that at least this part of human nature is common to all members of the species, regardless of their race or class and their undoubted differences in intellect, personality, and physical attributes. This belief is quite traditional (and Chomsky himself, we shall see, explicitly relates his views to those of the rationalist philosophers of the seventeenth and eighteenth centuries). What are new are the way in which Chomsky argues his case and the kind of evidence that he adduces in support of it.

It is appropriate, and symbolic of his position and influence, that the institution in which Chomsky carries out his research into the structure of language and the properties of the human mind should be that citadel of modern science, the Massachusetts Institute of Technology, but that the views he expresses in summarizing his research should be those more characteristic of the humanities departments of a traditional university. The contradiction is only apparent. For Chomsky's work suggests that the conventional boundary that exists between "arts" and "sciences" can, and should, be abolished.

Modern Linguistics: Aims and Attitudes

ii

For many readers of this book, possibly the majority, linguistics will be a completely new subject. I shall begin, therefore, by explaining in very general terms what linguistics is. We can then move on, in the next chapter, to consider those aspects of the subject that have been of particular importance in the formation of Chomsky's own thought.

Linguistics is commonly defined as the science of language. The word "science" is crucial here, and in our discussion of Chomsky's work we shall be very concerned with the implications of this term. For the moment, however, we may say that a *scientific* description is one that is carried out systematically on the basis of objectively verifiable observations and within the framework of some general theory appropriate to the data. It is often said that linguistics properly so called is of relatively recent origin and that the investigation of language as practiced in Europe and America before the nineteenth century was subjective, speculative, and unsystematic. Whether this sweeping condemnation of past linguistic research is historically justifiable is a question that we need not go into here. The important point to note is that linguistics as we know it today was developed in conscious opposition to the more traditional approaches to the study of language characteristic of earlier centuries. As we shall see, this deliberate break with the past was sharper and more definitive in America than it was in Europe. Nowhere was the rejection of traditional grammar more vehemently expressed than by the "Bloomfieldian" school of linguistics, dominant in the United States in the years following the Second World War— the school in which Chomsky was trained and against which, in due course, he reacted.

We shall not discuss here all the characteristics of modern linguistics that distinguish it from traditional grammar, but only those that are relevant to the theme of this book. The first of these, which is often regarded as a direct consequence of the scientific status of linguistics, is its *autonomy*, or independence of other disciplines. Traditional grammar, which like so much else in Western culture originated in Greece in the fifth century B.C., has since its beginnings been intimately connected with philosophy and literary criticism. At various times either the literary or the philosophical influence has been predominant, but they have both been present to some degree in all periods, and together they have shaped the attitudes and presuppositions with which scholars have for centuries approached the study of language. It is worth remembering also that these attitudes and presuppositions are now so pervasive and so deeply entrenched in our culture that not only the scholar trained in traditional grammar, but also the man in the street, tends to accept them without question. When the linguist claims "autonomy" for his subject he is asking to be allowed to take a fresh and objective look at language without prior commitment to traditional ideas and without necessarily adopting the same point of view as philosophers, psychologists, literary critics, or representatives of other disciplines. This does not mean that there is not, or should not be, any connection between linguistics and other disciplines concerned with language. Indeed, as we shall see in the later chapters of this book, there is at the present time a remarkable convergence of interest among linguists, psychologists, and philosophers. But the present rapprochement has come about as a consequence of the development of "autonomous" linguistics, and it is linguistics (more particularly, the work of Chomsky) that has provided the inspiration for the alliance of the three disciplines.

Reference has been made earlier to the literary bias of traditional grammar. That bias, which derived from the fact that the earliest Western grammarians were mainly concerned with the preservation and interpretation of the texts of the classical Greek writers, manifested itself in various ways. Scholars tended to concentrate upon the written language and to ignore the difference between speech and writing. Although the spoken language was not entirely neglected by traditional grammarians, it was only too often regarded as an imperfect copy of the written language. By contrast, most linguists today take it as axiomatic that speech is primary and that the written language is secondary and derived from it: in other words, that sound (more particularly, the range of sounds that can be produced by the so-called speech organs) is the *medium* in which language is "embodied" and that written languages result from the transference of speech to a secondary, visual medium. Every known language existed first as a spoken language, and thousands of languages have never, or only very recently, been committed to writing. Furthermore, children acquire a command of the spoken language before they learn to read and write; they do so spontaneously, without any training, whereas reading and writing are special skills in which the child is normally given special instruction based upon his prior knowledge of the corresponding spoken language. Although nothing will be said about phonetics in this book, and all the illustrative material will be cited in its normal written form, it must be constantly borne in mind that we are mainly concerned with the spoken language.

It should be emphasized that adherence to the principle of the primacy of speech over writing does not imply a lack of interest in, still less a contempt for, written languages. Nor does it necessarily imply (although many linguists, it must be admitted, have failed to make this qualification) that the written language is wholly derivative. The conditions in which the written language is used are different from the conditions in which the spoken language is employed: Since there is no face-to-face confrontation of reader and writer, information that is normally carried by the gestures and facial expressions accompanying speech and by a complex of other features that we may subsume here under the impressionistic term "tone of voice" must be conveyed in writing, if at all, by other means. The conventions of punctuation and the practice of italicizing words for emphasis are incapable of representing all the significant variations of pitch and stress that are present in spoken utterance. There will always be some degree of independence, therefore, in the written language. In many instances, as in the case of English, the difference between the spoken and written forms of the "same" language has been increased by the conservatism of the orthographic conventions, established some centuries ago and maintained to this day despite the changes that have since taken place in the pronunciation of the language in different parts of the world.

One further point should be made in this connection. It is often said that none of the "speech organs" has as its sole, or indeed its primary, function the part it plays in the production of speech—that the lungs are used in breathing, the teeth in the mastication of food, and so on—and that the "speech organs" do not constitute a physiological system in the normal sense of this term. It should not be forgotten, however, that the faculty of speech is as characteristic of human beings, and as natural and important to them, as walking on two feet, or even eating. Whatever may have been the cause of this, in some remote period of man's evolutionary development, it is a fact to be accounted for that all human beings make use of the same physiological "apparatus" in speech. It is at least conceivable that they are genetically "programed" to do so. The relevance of this point to the ideas of Chomsky will become clear in a later chapter.

Traditional grammarians were concerned more or less exclusively with the standard literary language; and they tended to disregard, or to condemn as "incorrect," informal or colloquial usage in both speech and writing. Also, they often failed to realize that the standard language was, from a historical point of view, merely that regional or social dialect that had acquired prestige and become the instrument of administration, education, and literature. Because of its more widespread use by a greater number of people and for a wider range of activities, the standard language may have acquired a richer vocabulary than any of the coexistent "substandard" dialects, but this has not made it intrinsically more correct.

The distinction between "language" and "dialect" is commonly drawn on political grounds. There is less difference between Swedish, Danish, and Norwegian, for example, which are usually referred to as distinct "languages," than there is between many of the so-called "dialects" of Chinese. The important point is that the regional or social dialects of a language, say, English, are no less systematic than the standard language and should not be described as imperfect approximations to it. This point is worth emphasizing, since many people are inclined to believe that it is only the standard language taught in school that is subject to systematic description. From a purely linguistic point of view, all the dialects of English are worthy of equal consideration.

Traditional grammar was developed on the basis of Greek and Latin, and it was subsequently applied, with minimal modifications and often uncritically, to the description of a large number of other languages. But there are many languages that, in certain respects at least, are strikingly different in structure from Latin, Greek, and the more familiar languages of Europe and Asia. One of the principal aims of modern linguistics has therefore been to construct a theory of grammar that is more *general* than the traditional theory—one that is appropriate for the description of all human languages and is not biased in favor of those languages that are similar in their grammatical structure to Greek and Latin.

One should perhaps mention at this point that linguistics provides no support for those who believe that there is a fundamental difference between "civilized" and "primitive" languages. The vocabulary of a language will, of course, reflect the characteristic pursuits and interests of the society that uses it. Any of the major world languages—English, French, Russian—will have a large number of words relating to modern science and technology that will have no equivalent in the language of some "underdeveloped" people. Conversely, however, there will be many words in the language of, let us say, some remote and backward tribe in New Guinea or South America that cannot be translated satisfactorily into English, French, or Russian, because these are words that refer to objects, flora, fauna, or customs unfamiliar in Western culture. The vocabulary of one language cannot be described as richer or poorer than the vocabulary of some other language in any absolute sense; every language has a sufficiently rich vocabulary for the expression of all the distinctions that are important in the society using it. We cannot therefore say, from this point of view, that one language is more "primitive" or more "advanced" than another. The point is even clearer with respect to the grammatical structure of languages. Differences there are between any particular "primitive" language and any particular "civilized" language. But these are no greater on the average than the differences between any random pair of "primitive" languages and any random pair of "civilized" languages. So-called primitive languages are no less systematic, and are neither structurally simpler nor structurally more complex, than the languages spoken by more "civilized" peoples. This is an important point. All human societies of which we have knowledge speak languages of roughly equal complexity, and the differences of grammatical structure that we do find among languages throughout the world are such that they cannot be correlated with the cultural development of the people speaking them and cannot be used as evidence for the construction of an evolutionary theory of human language. The uniqueness of language to the human species and the fact that no languages seem to be more primitive than any others, or closer to systems of animal communication, are points that have been given particular prominence in Chomsky's more recent work.

What are the features of human languages, then, that distinguish them from the systems of communication used by other species? This question will occupy us in greater detail later, but two particularly striking properties of human language may be mentioned here. The first of these is *duality of structure*. Every language so far investigated (and we may confidently assume that this will also be true of any language yet to come to the attention of linguists) has two *levels* of grammatical structure. There is, first of all, what we may call the "primary," or *syntactic*, level of analysis, at which sentences can be represented as combinations of meaningful units; we will call these *words* (and gloss over the fact that not all the minimal syntactic units in all languages are words in the usual sense of this term). And there is also a "secondary," or *phonological*, level, at which sentences can be represented as combinations of units that are themselves without meaning and serve for the identification of the "primary" units. The "secondary" units of language are sounds, or *phonemes* (to use a more technical term). If we take as an example the sentence *He went to London* (and, purely for the purpose of exposition, make the simplifying assumption that each letter represents one and only one phoneme), we can say that the sentence is composed of four words and that the first of these "primary" units is identified by the combination of the "secondary" units *h* and *e* (in that order), the second of the "primary" units by the combination *w*, *e*, *n*, and *t*, and so on. It should be noted that there is nothing that is particularly novel in the principle of duality of structure, as I have described it here. It was recognized in traditional grammar. But one point should be stressed. Although I have said that the "primary" units, unlike the "secondary" units, convey meaning (and this, in general at least, is true), it is not the defining characteristic of words that they have meaning. As we shall see, it is possible to analyze language at the syntactic level without reference to whether the units established at this level have meaning or not; and there are some words at least that have no meaning (e.g., *to* in *I want to go home*). We must be careful, therefore, not to describe the duality of structure that is being referred to here in terms of the association of sound and meaning.

Granted that every language manifests the property of duality of structure, we may expect that the description, or *grammar*, of every language will consist of three interrelated parts. The part that accounts for the regularities governing the combination of words is *syntax*. It is by means of syntactic rules, for example, that we specify that *He went to London*, by contrast with **Went to he London*,[1] is a grammatical sentence. The part of grammar that describes the meaning of words and sentences is *semantics*, and the part of grammar that deals with the sounds and their permissible combinations (e.g., the fact that *went*, but not **twne*, is a possible English word) is *phonology*.

At this point I should perhaps warn the reader that there is a certain amount of terminological confusion and inconsistency in linguistics. In the previous paragraph I have used the term "grammar" to refer to the whole of the systematic description of language, including both phonology and semantics, as well as syntax. This is the sense in which Chomsky uses the word "grammar" in his more recent writings; and I shall adhere to this usage throughout the present book, except in those sections where I explicitly draw the reader's attention to the fact that I am employing the term in a somewhat narrower sense. Many linguists describe as "grammar" what I am calling "syntax" and give a correspondingly restricted interpretation to "syntax" (opposing it to "morphology"). There are certain points of substance involved in the choice of terminology. But we need not go into these in this brief, and necessarily somewhat superficial, account of the

[1] The asterisk prefixed here indicates that this sequence of words is ungrammatical. I shall use this standard notational convention throughout.

aims and attitudes of modern linguistics. In this book we shall be mainly concerned with the theory of syntax, since this is the field where Chomsky has made his major contribution to the more technical side of linguistics.

The second general property of human language to be mentioned here is its *creativity* (or "open-endedness"). By this is meant the capacity that all native speakers of a language have to produce and understand an indefinitely large number of sentences that they have never heard before and that may indeed never have been uttered before by anyone. The native speaker's "creative" command of his language, it should be noted, is in normal circumstances unconscious and unreflecting. He is generally unaware of applying any grammatical rules or systematic principles of formation when he constructs either new sentences or sentences he has previously encountered. And yet the sentences that he utters will generally be accepted by other native speakers of the language as correct and will be understood by them. (We must make allowances, as we shall see later, for a certain amount of error—hence the qualification implied by "generally" in the previous sentence—but this does not affect the principle that is under discussion here.) As far as we know, this creative command of language is unique to human beings: It is *species-specific*. Systems of communication employed by species other than man are not "open-ended" in the same way. Most of them are "closed," in the sense that they admit of the transmission of only a finite and relatively small set of distinct "messages," the "meanings" of which are fixed (rather as the messages that one may send by means of the international telegraphic code are determined in advance), and it is not possible for the animal to vary these and construct new "sentences." It is true that certain forms of animal communication (for example, the signaling "code" that is used by bees to indicate the direction and distance of a source of honey) incorporate the possibility of making new "sentences" by systematically varying the "signal." But in all instances there is a simple correlation between the two variables—the "signal" and its "meaning." For example, as K. von Frisch discovered in his celebrated work on the subject, it is by the intensity of their body movements that bees signal the distance of the source of honey from the hive, and this parameter of "intensity" is subject to infinite (and continuous) variation. This kind of continuous variation is also found in human language; for instance, one can vary the "intensity" with which the word *very* is pronounced in a sentence like *He was very rich.* But it is not this feature that is being referred to when one talks of the creativity of human language. It is the ability to construct new combinations of discrete units, rather than simply to vary continuously one of the parameters of the signaling system in accordance with a correspondingly continuous variation in the "meaning" of the "messages." As we shall see in due course, Chomsky considers that the creativity of language is one of its most characteristic features and one that poses a particularly challenging problem for the development of a psychological theory of language use and language acquisition.

I have now introduced a number of the more important general principles that we shall take for granted, even when we do not draw explicitly upon them, in the following chapters. It may be helpful if I summarize them here. Modern linguistics claims to be more scientific and more general than traditional grammar. It assumes that the "natural" medium for the expression of language is sound (as produced by the speech organs) and that written languages are derived from speech. The grammar of any language will comprise at least the following three interrelated parts: syntax, semantics, and phonology; and it should, among other things, account for the ability native speakers have to produce and understand an indefinitely large number of "new" sentences.

What has been said in this chapter (due allowance being made for differences of emphasis) is neutral with respect to the theoretical differences that divide one school of linguistics from another at the present time. We now turn to a discussion of the "Bloomfieldian" (and "post-Bloomfieldian" or "neo-Bloomfieldian") school, in which, as I have said, Chomsky received his first training in linguistics.

The "Bloomfieldians"

iii

Linguistics in the United States has been very strongly influenced in this century by the necessity of describing as many as possible of the hundreds of previously unrecorded languages existing in North America. Since the publication of the *Handbook of American Indian Languages* in 1911, almost every linguist in America has, until very recently, included some original research on one or more of the American Indian languages as part of his training; and many of the features characteristic of American linguistics can be, in part at least, explained by this fact.

First of all, the experience of working with the indigenous languages of North America has given to a good deal of American linguistic theory its practical character and its sense of urgency. Many of these languages were spoken by very few people and would soon die out. Unless they were recorded and described before this happened, they would become forever inaccessible to investigation. In these circumstances, it is not surprising that American linguists have given considerable attention to the development of what are called "field methods"—techniques for the recording and analysis of languages that the linguist himself could not speak and that had not previously been committed to writing. There were no doubt other relevant factors (in particular, a certain interpretation of scientific rigor and objectivity), but the fact that linguistic theory was for many American scholars no more than a source of techniques for the description of previously unrecorded languages was at least partly to blame for what Chomsky was to condemn later as its concern with "discovery procedures."

Franz Boas (1858–1942), who wrote the Introduction to the *Handbook of American Indian Languages* (1911) and gave there an outline of the method he had himself worked out for their systematic description, came to the conclusion that the range of variation to be found in human languages was far greater than one might suppose if one based one's generalizations upon the grammatical descriptions of the more familiar languages of Europe. He found that earlier descriptions of the indigenous and "exotic" languages of the North American subcontinent had been distorted by the failure of linguists to appreciate the potential diversity of languages and their attempt to impose the traditional grammatical categories of description upon languages for which these were wholly inappropriate, and he pointed out that none of these traditional categories was necessarily present in all languages. To use two of Boas's examples: The distinction between singular and plural is not obligatory in Kwakiutl, so that *There is a house over there* and *There are some houses over there* are not necessarily distinguished; and the distinction between present and past tense is not made in Eskimo (*The man is coming* vs. *The man was coming*). Boas also gave examples of the converse situation, grammatical distinctions that were obligatory in certain American Indian languages but that were given no place at all in traditional grammatical theory: "Some of the Siouan languages classify nouns by means of particles, and strict distinctions are made between animate moving and animate at rest, animate long, inanimate high and inanimate collective objects." Examples like this were used by Boas to support the view that every language has its own unique grammatical structure and that the task of the linguist is to discover for each language the categories of description appropriate to it. This view may be called "structuralist" (in one of the many senses of a rather fashionable term).

It should be stressed that the "structuralist" approach was by no means confined to Boas and his successors in America. Similar views had been expressed by Wilhelm von Humboldt (1767–1835); and they were also expressed by European contemporaries of Boas, who were experienced, as he was, in the description of "exotic" languages. "Structuralism" has in fact been the rallying cry of many different twentieth-century schools of linguistics.

It would be universally agreed that the two greatest and most influential figures in American linguistics after Boas, in the period of the foundation of the Linguistic Society of America in 1924 to the beginning of the Second World War, were Edward Sapir (1884–1939) and Leonard Bloomfield (1887–1949). They were very different in temperament, in the range of their interests, in philosophical persuasion, and in the nature of the influence they exerted. Sapir had been trained in Germanic philology; but, while he was still a student, he came under the influence of Boas and turned to the study of American Indian languages. Like Boas, and like many American scholars down to the present day, he was an anthropologist as well as a linguist, and published widely in both fields. But Sapir's interests and professional competence extended beyond anthropology and linguistics, into literature, music, and art. He published a large number of articles and reviews (dealing with very many different languages), but only one book. This was a relatively short work, called *Language*, which appeared in 1921 and was addressed to the general reader. It is strikingly different, both in content and in style, from Bloomfield's *Language*, published twelve years later.

Bloomfield, as we shall see, did more than anyone else to make linguistics autonomous and scientific (as he understood the term "scientific"); and in the pursuit of this aim he was prepared to restrict the scope of the subject, excluding from consideration many aspects of language that, he believed, could not yet be treated with sufficient precision and rigor. Sapir, as one might expect from his other interests, took a more "humanistic" view of language. He laid great stress on its cultural importance, on the priority of reason over volition and emotion (emphasizing what he called "the prevailing cognitive character" of language), and on the fact that language was "purely human" and "noninstinctive."

Sapir's *Language*, though far shorter, is much more general and is easier to read (at a superficial level at least) than Bloomfield's. It is packed with brilliant analogies and suggestive comparisons, but Sapir's refusal to neglect any of the multifarious aspects of language gives to many of his theoretical statements, it must be admitted, an aura of vagueness that is absent from Bloomfield's book. Sapir's work has continued to hold the attention of linguists down to the present day. But there never has been a "Sapirian" school in the sense in which there has been, and still is, a "Bloomfieldian" school of linguistics in America. It is not surprising that this should be so. I shall say no more about Sapir, except to point out that many of the attitudes toward language that Sapir held are now held by Chomsky, although Chomsky's ideas have been developed in the "Bloomfieldian" tradition of "autonomous" linguistics.

As Bloomfield understood the term "scientific" (and this was a fairly common interpretation at the time), it implied the deliberate rejection of all data that were not directly observable or physically measurable. J. B. Watson, founder of the so-called behaviorist approach in psychology, took the same view of the aims and methodology of science. According to Watson and his followers, psychologists had no need to postulate the existence of the mind or of anything else that was not observable in order to explain those activities and capacities of human beings that were traditionally described as "mental" or "rational." The behavior of any organism, from an amoeba to a human being, was to be described and explained in terms of the organism's *response* to the *stimuli* presented by features of the environment. It was assumed that the organism's learning of these responses could be explained satisfactorily by means of the familiar laws of physics and chemistry, in much the same way as one might explain how a thermostat "learns" to respond to changes in temperature and to switch a furnace on or off.[1] Speech was but one among a number of forms of overt, or directly observable, behavior characteristic of human beings; and thought was merely inaudible speech ("talking with concealed musculature," as Watson put it). Since inaudible speech could be made audible, when neces-

[1] John Marshall has informed me that it is debatable whether the early behaviorists held such an extreme view as this. He suggests that Bloomfield's behaviorism was more radical than that of many of the psychologists who influenced him because he was himself a "convert" from mentalism. For a discussion of the historical background from this point of view, the reader is referred to Marshall's review of Esper's *Mentalism and Objectivism in Linguistics*.

sary, thought was in principle a form of observable behavior.

When Bloomfield came to write his monumental book *Language*, he explicitly adopted behaviorism as a framework for linguistic description.[2] In the second chapter he contrasted the traditional "mentalistic" explanation of language with "the *materialistic* (or, better, mechanistic) theory," according to which "human actions . . . are part of cause-and-effect sequences exactly like those we observe, say, in the study of physics or chemistry." He went on to claim that, although we could, in principle, foretell whether a certain stimulus would cause someone to speak and, if so, exactly what he would say, in practice we could make the prediction "only if we knew the exact structure of his body at the moment."[3] The meaning of a linguistic form was defined as "the practical events" with which the form "is connected," and, in a later chapter, as "the situation in which the speaker utters it and the response which it calls forth in the hearer."[4] As an example of a simple, but presumably typical, situation in which language might be used, Bloomfield suggested the following: Jack and Jill are walking down a lane; Jill sees an apple on a tree and, being hungry, asks Jack to get it for her; he climbs the tree and gives her the apple; and she eats it. This is the way in which we would normally describe the events that take place. A behavioristic account would run somewhat differently: Jill's being hungry ("that is, some of her muscles were contracting, and some fluids were being secreted, especially in her stomach") and her seeing the apple (that is, light waves reflected

---

[2] He had no less explicitly declared his adherence to the "mentalistic" psychology of Wundt in his earlier work *An Introduction to the Study of Language*.

[3] Bloomfield, *Language*, p. 33.

[4] *Ibid.*, pp. 27, 139.

from the apple reached her eyes) constitute the stimulus. The more direct response to this stimulus would be for Jill to climb the tree and get the apple herself. Instead, she makes a "substitute response" in the form of a particular sequence of noises with her speech organs; and this acts as a "substitute stimulus" for Jack, causing him to act as he might have done if he himself had been hungry and had seen the apple.

This behavioristic analysis of the situation obviously leaves a lot to be explained, but we shall not stop to discuss this question at this point. Bloomfield's fable will give the reader some idea of the way in which language was held to operate in practical situations as a substitute for other kinds of nonsymbolic behavior, and this is sufficient for our present purpose.

Bloomfield's commitment to behaviorism had no appreciable effect upon syntax or phonology in his own work or in that of his followers (except in so far as it fostered the development of an "empiricist" methodology; we shall come to this in due course). Bloomfield himself made reference to the behaviorist point of view only when he was dealing with meaning, and what he had to say on this topic was not calculated to inspire his followers with the desire to set about the construction of a comprehensive theory of semantics. It was Bloomfield's view that the analysis of meaning was "the weak point in language study" and that it would continue to be so "until human knowledge advances very far beyond its present state."[5] The reason for his pessimism lay in his conviction that a precise definition of the meaning of words presupposes a complete "scientific" description of the objects, states, processes, etc., to which they refer (i.e., for which they operate as "substitutes"). For a small number of words (the names of plants, animals, various natural substances, etc.) we were already in a position to give a reasonably precise definition by means of the technical terms of the relevant branch of science (botany, zoology, chemistry, etc.). But for the vast majority of words (Bloomfield gave examples like *love* and *hate*) this was not so. Bloomfield's attitude could not but discourage linguists from the study of meaning, and neither he nor his followers made any positive contribution whatsoever to the theory or practice of semantics. In fact, for almost thirty years after the publication of his book the study of meaning was wholly neglected by the "Bloomfieldian" school, and was frequently defined to be outside linguistics properly so called.

The "Bloomfieldian" attitude toward meaning, though stultifying as far as any progress in semantics was concerned, was not wholly detrimental to the development of other branches of linguistic theory. Bloomfield himself never suggested that it was possible to describe the syntax and phonology of a language in total ignorance of the meaning of words and sentences (although there can be little doubt that he would have thought this very desirable, if it were possible). His view was that for phonological and syntactic analysis it was necessary to know "whether two uttered forms were 'the same' or 'different,'" but that for this purpose all that was necessary was a rough-and-ready account of the meaning of words and not a full scientific description. Semantic considerations were strictly subordinated to the task of identifying the units of phonology and syntax and were not involved at all in the specification of the rules or principles governing their permissible combinations. This part of the grammar was to be a purely *formal* study, independent of semantics.

Bloomfield's followers carried even farther than he did the attempt to formulate the principles of phonological and syntactic analysis without reference to meaning. This effort reached its culmination in the work of Zellig Harris, notably in his *Methods in Struc-*

tural Linguistics, first published in 1951, though completed some years before. Harris's work also constituted the most ambitious and the most rigorous attempt that had yet been made to establish what Chomsky was later to describe as a set of "discovery procedures" for grammatical description.

Chomsky was one of Harris's pupils and later one of his collaborators and colleagues, and his earliest publications are very similar in spirit to those of Harris. By 1957, when Chomsky's first book, *Syntactic Structures*, was published, he had already moved away, as we shall see, from the position that Harris and the other "Bloomfieldians" had adopted on the question of "discovery procedures." But Chomsky continued to maintain that the phonology and syntax of a language could, and should, be described as a purely formal system without reference to semantic considerations. Language was an instrument for the expression of meaning; it was both possible and desirable to describe this instrument, in the first instance at least, without drawing upon one's knowledge of the use to which it was put. Semantics was part of the description of the use of language; it was secondary to and dependent upon syntax, and outside linguistics proper. In recent years Chomsky has become increasingly critical of "Bloomfieldian" linguistics and has abandoned many of the assumptions he originally held. It is worth emphasizing, therefore, not only that his earlier views were formed in the "Bloomfieldian" school but also that he could hardly have made the technical advances he did make in linguistics if the ground had not been prepared for him by such scholars as Harris.[6]

[6] For some further discussion of Chomsky's "Bloomfieldian" background, see Appendix 2.

The Goals of Linguistic Theory

iv

Before we move on to consider Chomsky's more technical contributions to linguistics, it will be as well to introduce and explain the motives and methodological assumptions that underlie his work. We shall concentrate mainly in this chapter on the account that Chomsky himself gives in his short but epoch-making book *Syntactic Structures*, published in 1957. As we shall see in due course, he takes a more comprehensive view of the scope of linguistics in his later works. Chapter 6 of *Syntactic Structures* bears the title "On the Goals of Linguistic Theory," which I have borrowed for my own chapter.

As I have already said, Chomsky's general views on linguistic theory as presented in *Syntactic Structures* are in most respects the same as those held by other members of the "Bloomfieldian" school, notably by Zellig Harris. In particular, it may be noted that there is no hint,

at this period, of the "rationalism" that is so characteristic a feature of Chomsky's more recent writing.
His acknowledgment of the influence of the "empiricist" philosophers Goodman and Quine would suggest that he shared their views, but there is no general
discussion in *Syntactic Structures* of the philosophical
and psychological implications of grammar.

However, there are one or two points that sharply
distinguish even Chomsky's earlier work from that of
Harris and the other "Bloomfieldians." In Chapter ii,
I mentioned that Chomsky lays great stress on the
creativity (or "open-endedness") of human language
and claims that the theory of grammar should reflect
the ability that all fluent speakers of a language possess
to produce and understand sentences they have never
heard before. As Chomsky came to realize later, earlier
scholars, including Wilhelm von Humboldt and Ferdinand de Saussure (1857–1913), had also insisted upon
the importance of this property of creativity. Actually,
it had been taken for granted, and occasionally mentioned explicitly, since the very beginnings of Western
linguistic theory in the ancient world. But it had been
neglected, if not denied, in "Bloomfieldian" formulations of the aims of linguistic theory. The reason for
this seems to have been that the "Bloomfieldians," in
common with many other twentieth-century schools
of linguistics, were very conscious of the need to distinguish clearly between *descriptive* and *prescriptive*
(or *normative*) grammar: between the description of
the rules that are actually followed by native speakers
and the prescription of rules that, in the opinion of
the grammarian, they ought to follow, in order to speak
"correctly." There are many examples of prescriptive
rules set up by grammarians that have no basis in the
normal usage of native speakers of English. (One such
instance is the rule that says that *It is I*, rather than
the more usual *It's me*, is "correct" English.) So concerned were the "Bloomfieldians" (and various other

"schools") with asserting the status of linguistics as a descriptive science that they made it a point of principle not to venture any judgments about the grammaticality, or "correctness," of sentences, unless these sentences had been attested in the usage of native speakers and included in the corpus of material that formed the basis of the grammatical description.

Chomsky insisted that the vast majority of the sentences in any representative corpus of recorded utterances would be "new" sentences, in the sense that they would occur once, and once only; and that this would remain true however long we went on recording utterances made by native speakers. The English language, like all the natural languages, consists of an indefinitely large number of sentences, only a small fraction of which have ever been uttered or will ever be uttered. The grammatical description of English may be based upon a corpus of actually attested utterances, but it will describe these, and classify them as "grammatical," only incidentally as it were, by "projecting" them onto the indefinitely large set of sentences that constitutes the language. Using Chomsky's terminology, we shall say that the grammar *generates* (and thereby defines as "grammatical") all the sentences of the language and does not distinguish between those that have been attested and those that have not.

The distinction that Chomsky draws in *Syntactic Structures* between the sentences generated by the grammar (the *language*) and a sample of the utterances produced, in normal conditions of use, by native speakers (the *corpus*) he draws in his later writings in terms of the notions of *competence* and *performance*. This terminological change is symptomatic of the evolution in Chomsky's thought from empiricism to rationalism, which has already been mentioned and will be discussed more fully later. In his later works, though not in *Syntactic Structures*, he stresses the fact that many of the utterances produced by native speakers (samples of their "performance") will, for various reasons, be ungrammatical. These reasons have to do with such linguistically irrelevant factors as lapses of memory or attention and malfunctions of the psychological mechanisms underlying speech. Given that this is so, it follows that the linguist cannot take the corpus of attested utterances at its face value, as part of the language to be generated by the grammar. He must *idealize* the "raw data" to some degree and eliminate from the corpus all those utterances that the native speaker would recognize, by virtue of his "competence," as ungrammatical. At first sight it might appear that Chomsky is here guilty of the confusion between description and prescription that was so common in traditional grammar. But this is not so. The view that all the utterances of a native speaker of a language are equally correct, and are proved to be so by the sole fact of their having been uttered— although it is a view that has often been maintained by linguists of an empiricist bent—is in the last resort untenable. And Chomsky is clearly right to claim for linguistics the same right to disregard some of the "raw data" as is accepted as normal in other sciences. There are, of course, serious problems, both practical and theoretical, involved in deciding what constitute extraneous or linguistically irrelevant factors; and it may well be that, in practice, the "idealization" of the data advocated by Chomsky does tend to introduce some of the normative considerations that marred much of traditional grammar. But this does not affect the general principle.

A further and related difference between Chomsky's earlier and later view of the "goals of linguistics" has to do with the role he assigns to the *intuitions*, or judgments, of native speakers. In *Syntactic Structures* he says that the sentences generated by the grammar should be "acceptable to the native speaker,"[1] and he considers that it is a point in favor of the kind of grammar he develops that it also accounts for the "intuitions" of native speakers with respect to the way certain sentences are recognized as equivalent or ambiguous. But the intuitions of the native speaker are presented as independent evidence, and their explanation is regarded as being secondary to the principal task of generating the sentences of the language. In later work Chomsky includes the intuitions of the speakers of a language as part of the data to be accounted for by the grammar. Furthermore, he now seems to place more reliance upon the validity and reliability of these intuitions than he did earlier, when he was much concerned with the need to test them by means of satisfactory "operational" techniques.

As we saw in the previous chapter, American linguistics in the "Bloomfieldian" period tended to be very "procedural" in orientation. Questions of theory were reformulated as questions of method ("How should one go about the practical task of analyzing a language?"); and it was commonly assumed that it should be possible to develop a set of procedures that, when applied to a corpus of material in an unknown language (or a language treated as if it were unknown to the linguist), would yield the correct grammatical analysis of the language of which the corpus was a representative sample. One of the main points argued by Chomsky in *Syntactic Structures* is that this is an unnecessary, and indeed harmful, assumption: "A linguistic theory should not be identified with a manual of useful procedures, nor should it be expected to provide mechanical procedures for the discovery of grammars."[2] The means by which a linguist arrives, in

[1] Chomsky, *Syntactic Structures*, pp. 49–50.
[2] *Ibid.*, p. 55, note 6.

practice, at one analysis rather than another might include "intuition, guess work, all sorts of partial methodological hints, reliance on past experience, etc."[3] What counts is the result, and this can be presented and justified without reference to the procedures that have been followed to achieve it. This does not mean that there is no point in trying to develop heuristic techniques for the description of languages, but simply —to put it crudely—that the proof of the pudding is in the eating. Just as the proof of a mathematical theorem can be checked without taking account of the way in which the person constructing the proof happened to hit upon the relevant intermediate propositions, so it should be with respect to grammatical analysis. As Chomsky says, the point would be granted immediately in the physical sciences, and there is no need for linguistics to set its sights higher than they do, especially as no linguist has yet come anywhere near formulating any satisfactory *discovery procedures*.

Linguistic theory should be concerned, then, with the justification of grammars. Chomsky goes on to consider the possibility of formulating criteria for deciding whether a particular grammar is the best one possible for the data. He concludes that even this goal —the formulation of a *decision procedure*—is too ambitious. The most that can be expected is that linguistic theory should provide criteria (an *evaluation procedure*) for choosing between alternative grammars. In other words, we cannot hope to say whether a particular description of the data is correct, in any absolute sense, but only that it is more correct than some alternative description of the same data.

Chomsky's distinction between decision procedures and evaluation procedures has caused a lot of misunderstanding and unnecessary controversy. After all, no physicist would say that Einstein's theory of rela-

3 *Ibid.*, p. 56.

tivity, for example, gives the best possible explanation of the data it covers, but only that it is better than the alternative theory, based on Newtonian physics, which it supplanted. Once again, why should linguistics set its sights higher than other sciences do? It is sometimes said that Chomsky's formulation of the goals of linguistic theory in terms of the comparison of alternative grammars glosses over the fact that for many languages we do not possess even a partial grammar and for no language do we have a grammar that is anywhere near being complete. This is indeed a fact. But the conclusion, that it is premature in these circumstances to talk of comparing grammars, does not follow. The construction of a set of grammatical rules involves the linguist in making decisions to handle the data in one way rather than another. Even if the rules describe only some small part of the data, there must be, whether explicit or implicit, a comparison of alternatives. It is the task of linguistic theory, says Chomsky, to make the alternatives explicit and to formulate general principles for deciding between them.

One further point should be made. Although Chomsky is, in one sense, proposing that linguistic theory should, in renouncing the "Bloomfieldian" quest for "discovery procedures," set itself a more modest goal than previously, there is a sense also in which his theoretical proposals are incomparably more ambitious than those of his predecessors. Some years before the publication of *Syntactic Structures*, in his little-known paper on "Systems of Syntactic Analysis," Chomsky had tried to formulate with mathematical precision some of the procedures of grammatical analysis outlined in Harris's *Methods in Structural Linguistics*. He was convinced by this experience, and by his examination of other "careful proposals for the development of linguistic theory," that the works in question, though apparently concerned with the specification of discovery procedures, in fact yielded "no more than evaluation procedures for grammars."[4] Chomsky's most original, and probably his most enduring, contribution to linguistics is the mathematical rigor and precision with which he formalized the properties of alternative systems of grammatical description. A fuller consideration of this topic must wait for the following chapters. Here I shall mention only one or two more general points.

At the very beginning of *Syntactic Structures*, Chomsky talks of a grammar as "a device of some sort for producing the sentences of the language under analysis." Chomsky's use of such words as "device" and "produce" in this context has misled many readers into thinking that he conceives of the grammar of a language in terms of some electronic or mechanical model—some piece of "hardware"—that replicates the behavior of the speaker of a language when he utters a sentence. It should be emphasized that he has employed these terms because the particular branch of mathematics that he has drawn upon in his formalization of grammar also uses such terms as "device," or even "machine," in a perfectly abstract way without reference to the physical properties of any actual model that might implement the abstract "device." This point will become clearer in the next chapter.

It is unfortunate, however, that Chomsky uses the word "produce" in the passage just cited. It almost inevitably suggests that the grammatical structure of the language is being described from the point of view of the speaker rather than the listener; that the grammar describes the production, and not the reception, of speech. There is a sense, as we shall see, in which a grammar of the kind developed by Chomsky does "produce" sentences by the application of a sequence of rules. But Chomsky has continually warned us against

[4] *Ibid.*, p. 52.

identifying the "production" of sentences within the grammar with the production of sentences by the speaker of a language. The grammar is intended to be neutral as between production and reception, to a certain extent explaining both, but no more biased toward one than it is toward the other. Chomsky does not usually talk of the grammar as "producing" sentences. The term he customarily employs is "generate," and this is the term that I used earlier in this chapter. But what exactly is meant by the word "generate" in this context?

We have already seen that a *generative* grammar is one that "projects" any given set of sentences upon the larger, and possibly infinite, set of sentences that constitute the language being described, and that it is this property of the grammar that reflects the creative aspect of human language. But "generative" for Chomsky has a second and equally important, if not more important, sense. This second sense, in which "generative" may be glossed as "explicit," implies that the rules of the grammar and the conditions under which they operate must be precisely specified. I can perhaps best illustrate what is meant by "generative" in this sense by means of a simple mathematical analogy (and Chomsky's use of the term "generate" does in fact derive from mathematical usage). Consider the following algebraic expression, or function: $2x + 3y - z$. Given that the variables x, y, and z can each take as its value one of the integers, the expression will generate (in terms of the usual arithmetical operations) an infinite set of resultant values. For example, with $x = 3$, $y = 2$, and $z = 5$, the result is 7; with $x = 1$, $y = 3$, and $z = 21$, the result is -10; and so on. We can say therefore that 7, -10, etc., are in the set of values generated by the function in question. If someone else applies the rules of arithmetic and obtains a different result, we say that he has made a mistake. We do not say that the rules are indeterminate and leave room for doubt at any point as to how they should be applied. Chomsky's conception of the rules of grammar is similar. They should be as precisely specified—*formalized* is the technical term—as the rules of arithmetic are. If we go on to identify the rules of the grammar with the native speaker's linguistic *competence*, as Chomsky does in his later work, we can account for the occurrence of ungrammatical sentences, and also for the occasional inability of listeners to analyze perfectly grammatical sentences, in much the same way as we can account for differences obtained in the evaluation of a mathematical function. We say that they are due to errors of *performance*—errors made in the application of the rules.

According to Chomsky, the grammar of a language should generate "all and only" the sentences of the language. If the reader is puzzled by the addition of "and only" (which is a relatively trivial instance of the kind of precision that is encouraged by formalization), he need only reflect that, by setting up the grammar in such a way that it generates every combination of English words (and this would be a very simple grammar), one would be sure of generating all the sentences of the language, but most of the combinations would not be sentences. The addition of "and only" is therefore an important qualification.

The generation of all and only the sentences of English, or any other language, might seem to be impossibly ambitious. It must be remembered, however, that this represents an ideal, which, even if it is impossible of fulfillment, is a goal toward which the grammarian of any language should continually work; and one grammar can be evaluated as better than another if, all other things being equal, it approximates more closely to this ideal. It should also be stressed, although this may appear somewhat paradoxical, that one is not committed by the adoption of Chomsky's ideal of generating all and only the sentences of the language to the view that the distinction between grammatical and ungrammatical sequences of words is invariably clear-cut, so that it is always possible to decide whether a given sequence should or should not be generated by the grammar. Chomsky points out in *Syntactic Structures* that it is a commonplace of the philosophy of science that, if a theory is formulated in such a way that it covers the clear cases, the theory itself can be used to decide the unclear cases. He advocates the same approach in linguistics, and for Chomsky a generative grammar is a scientific theory. To take a simple example (it is not one of Chomsky's): There are many speakers of English who would reject the putative sentence *The house will have been being built* and others who would accept it as quite normal. Since the judgments of native speakers do not seem to vary systematically with the dialects they speak, let us grant that, for English as a whole, the status of putative sentences like this is indeterminate (by contrast with the definitely acceptable *The house will have been built, The house is being built, They will have been building the house*, etc., and the definitely unacceptable **The house can will be built*, etc.). Since we do not know in advance whether *The house will have been being built* is a grammatical sentence or not, we can formulate the rules of the grammar to include all the definitely acceptable sequences and to exclude all the definitely unacceptable sequences and then see whether these rules exclude or include such sentences as *The house will have been being built*. (Sentences of this kind are in fact generated, and thereby defined as grammatical, by the rules given for English in *Syntactic Structures*.)

In this chapter we have confined our attention, for the most part, to Chomsky's earlier views on the aims and methodology of linguistics; and I have suggested that, except for his emphasis on the importance of creativity and his rejection of discovery procedures, when he wrote *Syntactic Structures* he was still very much a "Bloomfieldian." I have said that the most important and original part of Chomsky's earlier work lies in his formalization of various systems of generative grammar, and the next three chapters will be devoted to an account of this topic. We shall then take up the discussion of his more recent contributions to the psychology and philosophy of language.

Generative Grammar: a Simple Model

V

Our discussion of the more technical part of Chomsky's work will be relatively informal and will not presuppose any special training in, or aptitude for, mathematics. However, a sufficient number of terms and concepts will be introduced to give the reader some idea of the flavor of generative grammar and to make it possible for him to appreciate its significance. It should be pointed out that Chomsky's own treatment of generative grammar in *Syntactic Structures*, and indeed in most of his more accessible publications, is also fairly informal. But it rests upon a considerable amount of highly technical research, which he carried out in the years preceding the publication of *Syntactic Structures*. Much of this was described, in 1955, in a lengthy mimeographed monograph, "The Logical Structure of Linguistic Theory," which was made available to interested scholars and university libraries but has only recently been published. (See Appendix 2.)

In this chapter we shall be dealing with a very simple formal system, the first of the "three models for the description of language" discussed by Chomsky in *Syntactic Structures* and elsewhere—one that he very quickly proved was insufficiently powerful for the syntactic analysis of English and other natural languages. I shall first introduce a number of terms and concepts that will be required, not only here but also for the discussion of the more complex models of grammar in the next two chapters. Throughout these three chapters I shall assume an intuitive knowledge of at least some of the sentences of English that we should definitely wish to regard as well formed, or *grammatical*, and of at least some of the sequences of words that we should definitely wish to classify as ill-formed, or *ungrammatical*. How we have come by this knowledge and how we might go about putting it to the test are important questions, but they are irrelevant to the formalization of linguistic description, which is our present concern.

We may begin by defining the *language* that is described by a particular grammar as the set of all the sentences it generates. The set of sentences may be, in principle, either finite or infinite in number. But English (and as far as we know all other natural languages) comprises an infinite (i.e., indefinitely large) number of sentences, because there are sentences and phrases in the language that can be extended indefinitely and will yet be accepted as perfectly normal by native speakers. Obvious examples are sentences like *This is the man that married the girl that . . .* (sentences of the "House-that-Jack-built" type) and phrases like *large, black, three-cornered . . . hat*, which can be expanded to any desired length by making appropriate insertions in place of the three dots. Obviously, there are certain practical limitations upon the length of any sentence that has ever been, or will ever be, uttered by native speakers of English. But the point is that no *definite* limit can be set to the length of English sentences. We must, therefore, accept that, in theory, the number of grammatical sentences in the language is infinite.

But the number of words in the vocabulary of English is, we will assume, finite. There is a considerable variation in the words known to different native speakers, and there may well be some difference between the "active" and the "passive" vocabulary of every individual (i.e., between the words he will himself use as a speaker and the words he will recognize and understand if someone else uses them). Indeed, neither the "active" nor the "passive" vocabulary of any native speaker of English is fixed and static even for relatively short periods of time. We shall, however, discount these facts in our discussion of the grammar of English and assume, for simplicity, that the vocabulary of the language is both determinate and invariable, and of course finite.

We shall also assume that the distinct operations that are involved in the generation of English sentences are finite in number. There is no reason to believe that this is an implausible assumption; and if they were not, this would mean that the sentences of English could not be generated by means of a specifiable set of rules. Now, if the grammar is to consist of a finite set of rules operating upon a finite vocabulary and is to be capable of generating an infinite set of sentences, it follows that at least some of the rules must be applicable more than once in the generation of the same sentence. Such rules, and the structures they generate, are called *recursive*. Once again, there is nothing implausible in the suggestion that the grammar of English should include a certain number of recursive rules. It is intuitively clear that, in expanding the sentence *This is the man that married the girl* by adding to it the clause *that wrote the book,* a clause of the same type as *that married the girl* has been added to the original sentence.

Sentences can be represented, as we saw in Chapter ii, at two *levels*: at the syntactic level as sequences of words and at the phonological level as sequences of phonemes. It would be possible, in principle, to consider the syntactic structure of sentences as something that is totally or partially independent of the order in which the words occur relative to one another; and certain languages, with what is described as "free word order," have been traditionally described from this point of view. However, following Chomsky, we shall make it a matter of definition that every different sequence of words (if it is well formed) is a different sentence. Under this definition, not only are *The dog bit the man* and *The man bit the dog* different sentences, but so also are *I had an idea on my way home* and *On my way home I had an idea.*

From the purely syntactic point of view, the phonological structure of words is irrelevant; and we could represent them in any one of a variety of ways. For instance, we could list all the words in the vocabulary in some arbitrary order, number them according to their place on the list, and then use these numbers to denote particular words in the syntactic description of sentences. It is the usual practice, however, to represent words as sequences of phonemes (or letters) even at the syntactic level; and we shall follow this practice. We shall, in fact, cite words and syntactic units in their normal orthographic form, but the reader should bear in mind that the spelling or pronunciation of words is, in principle, independent of their identity as syntactic units. It is generally accepted that two different words can be written or pronounced in the same way and that there can be alternative ways of spelling or pronouncing the same word.

We shall now introduce a distinction between "terminal" and "auxiliary" elements. *Terminal elements* are those that actually occur in sentences: words at the syntactic level and phonemes at the phonological level. All other terms or symbols that are employed in the formulation of grammatical rules may be described as *auxiliary elements*. In particular, it should be noted that the terms or symbols used to denote the "parts of speech" are auxiliary elements in generative grammars of the kind we shall be considering. We shall use familiar traditional terms for word classes, or "parts of speech," as Chomsky does, and abbreviate them symbolically: N = Noun, V = Verb, etc. Other auxiliary elements will be introduced later. One point that should be stressed here is that in a generative grammar the fact that a particular word belongs to a particular class—that it is a member of the class N, let us say—must be made perfectly explicit within the grammar. In effect this means, in grammars of the type formalized by Chomsky, that every word in the vocabulary must be assigned to the syntactic class, or classes, to which it belongs; it will not be sufficient to draw up a set of definitions, such as "A noun is the name of any person, place, or thing," and then leave it to the person referring to the grammar to decide whether a particular word satisfies the definition or not.

The simplest grammars discussed by Chomsky that are capable of generating an infinite set of sentences by means of a finite number of recursive rules operating upon a finite vocabulary are what he calls *finite-state grammars*. These are based on the view that sentences are generated by means of a series of choices made "from left to right"; that is to say, after the first, or leftmost, element has been selected, every subsequent choice is determined by the immediately preceding elements. According to this conception of syntactic structure, a sentence like *This man has brought some bread* might be generated as follows. The word *this* would be selected for the first position from a list of all the words capable of occurring at the beginning of English sentences. Then *man* would be selected as one of the words possible after *this*; *has*, as one of the words that can occur after *this* and *man*; and so on. If we had selected *that*, instead of *this*, for the first position, the subsequent choices would have been un-affected: *That man has brought some bread* is an equally acceptable sentence. On the other hand, if we had first selected *those* or *these*, we should then have to select words like *men* for the second position, followed by words like *have* for the third position—the possibilities for the fourth and subsequent positions being as before. And if we had selected *the* initially, we could continue with either *man* and *has* or *men* and *have*. One way of representing graphically what has just been said in words is by means of the "state diagram" shown in Figure 1. (I have deliberately used a slightly more complicated example than the one Chomsky gives on page 19 of *Syntactic Structures*.)

The diagram may be interpreted as follows. We can think of the grammar as a machine, or device (in the abstract sense explained in the previous chapter), which moves through a finite number of internal "states" as it passes from the *initial state* ("start") to the *final state* ("stop") in the generation of sentences. When it has produced (let us say, "printed out" or "emitted") a word (from the set of words given as possible for that "state") the grammar then "switches" to a new state as determined by the arrows. Any sequence of words that can be generated in this way is thereby defined to be grammatical (in terms of the grammar represented by the diagram).

The grammar illustrated in Figure 1 will generate, of course, only a finite number of sentences. It can be extended, however, by allowing the device to "loop" back to the same or some previous state at particular points of choice. For example, we could add "loops" between {*this, that, the, some, a, . . .*} and {*man, bread,*

book, . . .} and between *{these, those, the, some, . . .}*
and *{men, books, . . .}* making possible the selection
of one or more elements from the set *{awful, fat,
big, . . .},* and thus the generation of sentences beginning *That awful man, That big fat man, Some big fat
awful men,* etc. The grammar could also be extended
in an obvious way to allow for the generation of compound sentences like *That man has brought us some
bread and this beautiful girl has eaten the cheese.*

FIGURE I

These sentences are still very simple in structure;
and it would clearly be a complicated matter, even if
it were possible, to construct a finite-state grammar
capable of generating a large and representative
sample of the sentences of English. It will be observed,
for example, that we have had to put *the* both with
this, that, etc., and with *these, those,* etc. We would

also have to put {*awful, fat, big,* ...} in several different places, because *this awful man* and *these awful men*, but not *these awful man and *this awful men, are acceptable. Problems of this kind would multiply very quickly if we seriously set about the task of writing a finite-state grammar for English, and the conception of syntactic structure that underlies this model of description has little to recommend it other than its formal simplicity. But Chomsky proved that our rejection of finite-state grammar as a satisfactory model for the description of natural language is more solidly based than it would be if it rested solely upon considerations of practical complexity and our intuitions as to how certain grammatical phenomena ought to be described. He demonstrated the inadequacy of finite-state grammars by pointing out that there are certain regular processes of sentence formation in English that cannot be accounted for at all, no matter how clumsy or counterintuitive an analysis we were prepared to tolerate, within the framework of finite-state grammar.

Chomsky's proof of the inadequacy of finite-state grammar[1] rests upon the fact that there may be dependencies holding between nonadjacent words and that these interdependent words may themselves be separated by a phrase or clause containing another pair of nonadjacent interdependent words. For example, in a sentence like *Anyone who says that is lying* there is a dependency between the words *anyone* and *is lying*. They are separated by the simple clause *who says that* (in which there is a dependency between *who* and *says*). We can easily construct more complex examples, e.g., *Anyone who says that people who deny that* ... *are wrong is foolish.* Here we have dependencies between *anyone* and *is foolish*, and between *people* and *are wrong*; and we can go on to insert between *that*

[1] Chomsky, *Syntactic Structures*, pp. 21–24.

and *are* a clause that itself contains nonadjacent inter-dependent words. The result is a sentence with "mirror-image properties"—that is to say, a sentence of the form $a + b + c \ldots x + y + z$, where there is a relationship of compatibility or dependency between the outermost constituents (a and z), between the next outermost (b and y), and so on. Any language that contains an indefinitely large number of sentences with "mirror-image properties" like this is beyond the scope of finite-state grammar.

As I have said, the generation of sentences by means of a series of choices made "from left to right" has little to recommend it other than the formal simplicity of the model. The reason why Chomsky paid any attention at all to finite-state grammar is that language had been considered from this point of view in connection with the design of efficient channels of communication during the Second World War; and the highly sophisticated mathematical theory of communication that resulted ("information theory") was extended to many fields, including psychology and linguistics, after the war. Chomsky did not prove, or claim to prove, that "information theory," as such, was irrelevant to the investigation of language, but merely that, if it were applied on the assumption of "word-by-word" and "left-to-right" generation, it could not handle some of the constructions in English.

Phrase Structure Grammar

vi

In the previous chapter we made the tacit assumption that the syntactic structure of a sentence could be fully accounted for by specifying the words of which the sentence was composed and the order in which they occurred. We saw that a finite-state grammar, based on this assumption, was incapable of generating certain sentences of English. The second of Chomsky's "three models for the description of language," phrase structure grammar, is much more satisfactory from this point of view. Any set of sentences that can be generated by a finite-state grammar can be generated by a phrase structure grammar. But the converse does not hold: There are sets of sentences that can be generated by a phrase structure grammar but not by a finite-state grammar. This was one of the theorems that Chomsky proved in the more technical work that preceded the publication of *Syntactic Structures*.

Let us express the relationship between phrase structure grammars and finite-state grammars by saying that phrase structure grammars are intrinsically more *powerful* than finite-state grammars. (They can do everything that finite-state grammars can do—and more.)

Consider the following English sentence (I have here taken one of Chomsky's own examples): *The man hit the ball*. It is made up of five words arranged in a particular order. I shall refer to the words out of which the sentence is composed as its *ultimate constituents* (implying that these elements are not further analyzable at the syntactic level). The order in which the ultimate constituents occur relative to one another may be described as the *linear structure* of the sentence. Now, linguists have generally claimed that sentences have another kind of syntactic structure in addition to, or independent of, their linear structure. A traditionally minded grammarian might say, of our simple model sentence, that (like all simple sentences) it has a *subject* and a *predicate*; that the subject is a *noun phrase* (*NP*), which consists of the *definite article* (*T*) and a *noun* (*N*); and that the predicate is a *verb phrase* (*VP*), which consists of a *verb* (*V*) with its *object*, which, like the subject, is a noun phrase consisting of the definite article and a noun. Essentially the same kind of description would have been given by "Bloomfieldian" linguists in terms of the notions of *immediate constituent analysis*: The "immediate constituents" of the sentence (the two phrases into which it can be analyzed at the first stage) are the noun phrase *the man* (which has the role, or *function*, of subject) and the verb phrase *hit the ball* (which has the function of predicate); the immediate constituents of *the man* are the article *the* and the noun *man*; the immediate constituents of *hit the ball* are the verb *hit* and the noun phrase *the ball* (which has the function of object); and the immediate con-

stituents of *the ball* are the article *the* and the noun
ball.

The notion of constituent structure, or *phrase structure* (to use Chomsky's term), is comparable to the
notion of "bracketing" in mathematics or symbolic
logic. If we have an expression of the form $x \times (y + z)$, we know that the operation of addition must
be carried out first and the operation of multiplication
afterward. By contrast, $x \times y + z$ is interpreted (by
means of the general convention that, in the absence
of brackets, multiplication takes precedence over addition) as being equivalent to $(x \times y) + z$. Generally
speaking, the order in which the operations are carried
out will make a difference to the result. For instance,
with $x = 2$, $y = 3$, and $z = 5$: $x \times (y + z) = 16$,
whereas $(x \times y) + z = 11$. There are many words in
English and other languages that are ambiguous in
much the same way that $x \times y + z$ would be ambiguous if it were not for the prior adoption by mathematicians of the general convention that multiplication
takes precedence over addition. A classic example is
the phrase *old men and women* (and more generally
A N and N), which may be interpreted either as (*old
men*) *and women*—cf., $(xy) + z$; or *old* (*men and
women*)—cf., $x(y + z)$. Under the first interpretation
the adjective *old* applies only to *men*; under the second
interpretation it applies both to *men* and to *women*.
With the phrase structure indicated, by means of
brackets, as *old {men and women}* the string of words
we are discussing is semantically equivalent to (*old
men*) *and* (*old women*)—cf., $x(y + z) = (xy) + (xz)$. I shall not pursue the mathematical analogy
beyond this point. For our present purpose, it is sufficient to note that two strings of elements may have the
same linear structure but differ with respect to their
phrase structure, and that the difference in their
phrase structure may be semantically relevant.

The theoretical importance of this phenomenon,

which we may refer to as *structural ambiguity* (Chomsky's term in *Syntactic Structures* is "constructional homonymity"), lies in the fact that the ambiguity of such strings as *old men and women* cannot be accounted for by appealing to a difference in the meaning of any of the ultimate constituents or to a difference of linear structure.

The theory of immediate constituent analysis had been much discussed by Chomsky's predecessors. Chomsky's major contribution with respect to this model of syntactic structure was first of all to show how it could be formalized by means of a system of generative rules and then to demonstrate that, although phrase structure grammar was more powerful and more satisfactory for the description of natural languages that finite-state grammar, it had certain limitations. Chomsky's formalization of phrase structure grammar may be illustrated by means of the following rules (which, with minor modifications, are identical with those given in *Syntactic Structures*):

(1) *Sentence* → *NP* + *VP*
(2) *NP* → *T* + *N*
(3) *VP* → *Verb* + *NP*
(4) *T* → *the*
(5) *N* → {*man, ball, . . .*}
(6) *Verb* → {*hit, took, . . .*}

This set of rules (which will generate only a small fraction of the sentences of English) is a simple phrase structure grammar.

Each of these rules is of the form $X \rightarrow Y$, where X is a single element and Y is a *string* consisting of one or more elements. The arrow is to be interpreted as an instruction to replace the element that occurs to its left with the string of elements that occurs to its right ("rewrite" X as Y). Rules 5 and 6 employ brace brackets to list a set of elements any one of which, but only one of which, may be selected. (In each case only two members of the set have been given; the dots can be read as "etc.") The rules are to be applied as follows. We start with the element *Sentence* and apply Rule 1; this yields the *string* (i.e., sequence of symbols; "string" is a technical term) *NP + VP*. We inspect this string to see whether any of the elements occurring in it can be rewritten by means of Rules 1–6. It will be seen that either Rule 2 or Rule 3 can be applied at this point; it does not matter which we select. Applying Rule 3, we get the string *NP + Verb + NP*. We can now apply Rule 2 twice, followed by Rules 4 and 5 twice, and Rule 6 once (in any order except that Rule 2 must precede Rules 4 and 5, as Rule 3 must precede Rule 6 and one of the applications of Rule 2). The *terminal string* generated by the rules (assuming that *man, hit,* and *ball* are selected at the appropriate points) is *the + man + hit + the + ball,* and it takes nine steps to generate this string of words. The set of nine strings, including the initial string, the terminal string, and seven intermediary strings constitutes a *derivation* of the sentence *The man hit the ball* in terms of this particular phrase structure grammar. (The reader may wish to check his understanding of the rules by constructing a sample derivation himself.)

But how does this system assign to sentences the appropriate phrase structure? The answer to this question is given by a convention associated with the operation of "rewriting." Whenever we apply a rule we put brackets, as it were, around the string of elements that is introduced by the rule, and we label the string within the brackets as an instance of the element that has been rewritten by the rule. For example, the string *NP + VP* derived by Rule 1 is bracketed and labeled as *Sentence (NP + VP)*. The labeled bracketing assigned to *NP + Verb + NP* is *Sentence (NP + VP (Verb + NP))*, and so on. An alternative, and equivalent, means of representing the labeled bracketing assigned to strings of elements generated by a phrase structure grammar is a *tree diagram*, as illustrated for our model sentence in Figure 2. Since tree diagrams are visually clearer than sequences of symbols and brackets, they are more commonly used in the literature, and I shall employ them (except for very simple instances) in what follows. The labeled bracketing, associated with a terminal string generated by a phrase structure grammar, is called a *phrase marker*.

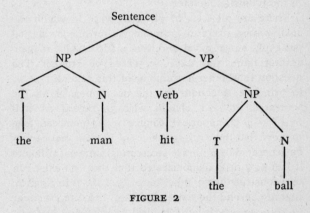

FIGURE 2

It will be obvious that the phrase marker given in Figure 2 conveys directly the following information: the string of terminal elements *the + man + hit + the + ball* is a *Sentence* that consists of two constituents, *NP* (*the man*) and *VP* (*hit the ball*); the *NP* that occurs to the left of *VP* consists of two constituents, *T* (*the*) and *N* (*man*); *VP* consists of two constituents, *Verb* (*hit*) and *NP* (*the ball*); and the *NP* that occurs to the right of *Verb* consists of two constituents, *T* (*the*) and *N* (*ball*). It thus represents all that I said earlier might have been considered relevant in an immediate constituent analysis of the sentence, except for the fact that *the man* is the

subject, *hit the ball* is the predicate, and *the ball* is
the object. But these notions, and in particular the
distinction between the subject and the object, can
also be defined in terms of the associated phrase
marker.[1] The *subject* is the NP that is directly dominated by *Sentence*, and the object is the NP that is
directly dominated by VP. What is meant by "domina-
tion" should be clear, without formal definition, from
the tree diagrams. We shall need to appeal to this
notion in our discussion of transformational grammar
in the following chapter.

There are all sorts of different ways in which the
small phrase structure grammar with which we started
out could be extended and thus made capable of generating more and more sentences of English. The
question is whether a grammar of this general type is,
in principle, adequate for the description of all the
sentences that we should wish to regard as well
formed, or grammatical. Chomsky has not been able
to prove that there are sentences of English that cannot
be generated by a phrase structure grammar (although
it has now been demonstrated that there do exist certain constructions in other languages, if not in English,
that are beyond the scope of phrase structure grammar
in this sense). What Chomsky claims, in *Syntactic
Structures* and elsewhere, is that there are sentences
of English that can be described only "clumsily" within
the framework of phrase structure grammar—that is
to say, in a way that is "extremely complex, *ad hoc*,
and 'unrevealing.'"

The important point to note is that Chomsky here
allows for the possibility that, although two grammars
may be equivalent in the sense that they each generate
the same set of sentences (I shall refer to this as *weak*

[1] As Chomsky suggests in *Syntactic Structures*, p. 30, and
makes explicit later, notably in *Aspects of the Theory of
Syntax*, p. 71.

equivalence), there may yet be good reasons for considering one grammar to be preferable to the other. In
Syntactic Structures, Chomsky claims that one of the
main reasons for preferring a transformational grammar to a phrase structure grammar is that the former
is, in a certain sense, simpler than the latter. It has
proved very difficult, however, to make formally precise
the sense in which the term "simplicity" is being
employed here. How do we decide, for example, that a
grammar that requires relatively few rules, some of
which, however, are quite complex, for the generation
of a given set of sentences is, as a whole, more or less
"simple" than a second, weakly equivalent, grammar
that requires far more rules, none of which, however,
is particularly complex, to generate the same set of
sentences? There is no obvious way of balancing one
kind of simplicity against another.

In his later publications Chomsky attaches far less
importance to the notion of "simplicity," and gives
correspondingly more weight to the argument that
transformational grammar reflects better the "intuitions" of the native speaker and is semantically more
"revealing" than phrase structure grammar.[2] I can
illustrate the deficiencies of phrase structure grammar
from this point of view with reference to the generation

[2] Chomsky tells me that he is not himself aware of any
change in his attitude over the years with respect to the
role of simplicity measures and intuition. He thinks that
some confusion may have been caused by the fact that
Syntactic Structures was "a rather watered-down version of
earlier work (at that time unpublishable)" and that, for
this reason, it "emphasized weak rather than strong generative capacity." I am sure that most linguists who read
Syntactic Structures when it was first published in 1957
interpreted Chomsky's general views on linguistic theory
in the way that I have represented them in Chapter iv.
One can only wonder whether Chomsky's work would have
had the effect that it did have within linguistics if *Syntactic
Structures* had not been "watered down." (But see now
Appendix 2.)

of corresponding active and passive sentences in English, e.g., *The man hit the ball* and *The ball was hit by the man*. We have already seen how active sentences might be generated in a phrase structure grammar, and we could easily add further rules to the system in order to generate passive sentences. What we cannot represent within the framework of a phrase structure grammar, however, is the fact (and let us grant that it is a fact) that pairs of sentences like *The man hit the ball* and *The ball was hit by the man* are "felt" by native speakers to be related, or to "belong" together in some way, and to have the same or a very similar meaning. As we shall see in the following chapter, this relationship between corresponding active and passive sentences, as well as many other "intuitive" and semantic relationships, *can* be accounted for in a transformational grammar.

All the phrase structure rules introduced in this chapter so far have been *context-free*; that is to say, they have all been of the form $X \to Y$, where X is a single element and Y is a string of one or more elements, no reference being made to the context in which X is to be rewritten as Y. Consider, by contrast, a rule of the following form: $X \to Y/W - V$ (to be read as "X is to be rewritten as Y in the context of W to the left and V to the right"—there are various ways in which the contextual restrictions may be indicated). It is by means of a *context-sensitive* rule, cast in this form, that we might wish to account for the "agreement," or concord, that holds between the subject and the verb in English sentences (cf., *The boy runs*, but *The boys run*) and for similar phenomena in other languages; and we shall make use of context-sensitive rules in the next chapter. Here we may simply note that, from the formal point of view, context-free grammars can be regarded as a special subclass of context-sensitive grammars, this subclass being defined by the property that in each of the rules $X \to Y/W - V$

the contextual variables W and V are left "empty." It may be added that any set of sentences that can be generated by a context-free grammar can be generated by a context-sensitive grammar; the converse, however, is not true.

The statement that has just been made, which implies that context-sensitive grammars are intrinsically more powerful than context-free grammars (as context-free phrase structure grammars are intrinsically more powerful than finite-state grammars), illustrates again a very important, but highly technical, aspect of Chomsky's work, which I can do no more than mention in a book of this kind. The study of the formal properties and generative capacity of various types of grammar exists as a branch of mathematics or logic, independently of its relevance for the description of natural languages. The revolutionary step that Chomsky has taken, as far as linguistics is concerned, has been to draw upon this branch of mathematics (finite automata theory and recursive function theory) and to apply it to natural languages, like English, rather than to the artificial languages constructed by logicians and computer scientists. But he has done more than simply take over and adapt for the use of linguists an existing system of formalization and a set of theorems proved by others. He has made an independent and original contribution to the study of formal systems from a purely mathematical point of view. The mathematical investigation of phrase structure grammars, and more particularly of context-free phrase structure grammar, is now well advanced; and various degrees of equivalence have been proved between phrase structure grammar and other kinds of grammar, which also formalize the notion of "bracketing," or immediate constituent structure. So far the mathematical investigation of transformational grammar, which was initiated by Chomsky, has made relatively little progress. But a transformational grammar, as we shall see in the next chapter, is a far more complex system than phrase structure grammar (although it may well be the case, as Chomsky claims in *Syntactic Structures*, that it yields a "simpler" description of certain sentences).[3]

[3] For a rather more formal treatment of the basic concepts of generative grammar, reference may be made to Appendix 1.

Transformational Grammar

vii

We shall not go into a great deal of detail in our discussion of transformational grammar. However, it is impossible to understand Chomsky's more general views on the philosophy of language and mind unless one has some knowledge of the principal characteristics of the system of grammatical description that he founded some twenty years ago and that has been under more or less continuous development since that time.

The first point that must be made is terminological. Whereas a phrase structure grammar is one that consists solely of phrase structure rules, a transformational grammar (as originally conceived by Chomsky) does not consist only of transformational rules. It includes a set of phrase structure rules as well. The transformational rules depend upon the previous application of the phrase structure rules and have the effect not only of converting one string of elements into another but, in principle, of changing the associated phrase marker. Furthermore, they are formally more heterogeneous and more complex than phrase structure rules. I shall give some examples of transformational rules presently, but I must first introduce an appropriate set of phrase structure rules.

We will use those given by Chomsky[1]—with one or two minor changes:

(1) *Sentence* → NP + VP
(2) *VP* → *Verb* + NP
(3) *NP* → $\left\{ \begin{array}{l} NP_{sing} \\ NP_{pl} \end{array} \right\}$
(4) NP_{sing} → T + N
(5) NP_{pl} → T + N + s
(6) *T* → *the*
(7) *N* → {*man, ball, door, dog, book, . . .*}
(8) *Verb* → *Aux* + V
(9) *V* → {*hit, take, bite, eat, walk, open, . . .*}
(10) *Aux* → *Tense* (+ M) (+ *have* + *en*) (+ *be* + *ing*)
(11) *Tense* → $\left\{ \begin{array}{l} Present \\ Past \end{array} \right\}$
(12) *M* → {*will, can, may, shall, must*}

It will be observed that this set of rules allows for a wider range of choices than those given in the previous chapter. Both singular and plural noun phrases are accounted for, by Rule 3; and a large number of tenses and moods are introduced (instead of just the simple past tense of *The man hit the ball*) by means of the element *Aux* and its subsequent development. Rule 10 implies that every string generated by it must contain the element *Tense* and may contain, in addition, one or more of the other strings of elements in brackets. (Elements like s in Rule 5 and *en* or *ing* in Rule 10 are

[1] *Syntactic Structures*, p. 111.

morphemes rather than words. In fact, *have, be, the*, and all the elements listed on the right-hand side of Rules 7, 9, and 12 may also be regarded as morphemes. But we need not dwell here upon the difference between a "word" and a "morpheme" in linguistic theory.)

Assuming that the lists given in Rules 7 and 9 are considerably extended, this system of phrase structure rules will generate a large (but finite) number of what we may call *underlying strings*. It should be emphasized that an underlying string (as indeed will be evident from the above rules) is not a sentence. The transformational rules have yet to be applied. One of the strings generated by these rules is *the + man + Present + may + have + en + open + the + door* (which, given the transformational rules of *Syntactic Structures*, underlies both the active sentence *The man may have opened the door* and the corresponding passive *The door may have been opened by the man*). The reader may wish to verify that this string is indeed generated by the rules and to construct the associated phrase marker.

Chomsky derived passive sentences from underlying strings in *Syntactic Structures* by means of an optional rule, which we may give, rather informally, as follows:

(13) $NP_1 + Aux + V + NP_2 \rightarrow NP_2 + Aux + be + en + V + by + NP_1$

This rule differs in various respects from the phrase structure rules. Not just one element, but a string of four elements, appears to the left of the arrow; and the operation that is carried out by the rule is quite complex—involving the permutation of the two *NP*s (this is indicated by the subscripts) and the insertion of the elements *be, en*, and *by* at particular points.

There is, however, an even more important difference between the phrase structure rules (1–12) and the transformational rule (13); and this has to do with the way in which we interpret the symbols that occur in the rules. In a phrase structure rule a single symbol designates one and only one element in the string to which the rule applies. But in a transformational rule a single symbol may refer to a string of more than one element, provided that the string in question is *dominated* by (i.e., "derived from"; see pages 65–66) this symbol in the associated phrase marker. It is in this sense that transformational rules are said to operate upon phrase markers rather than simply upon strings of elements.

I shall first of all illustrate what is meant by this statement with reference to a purely abstract example. Given that the string $a + d + e + b + f + c + g + h$ has been generated by a set of phrase structure rules that assign to it the phrase marker illustrated in Figure 3 (the reader can easily reconstruct these rules for himself), this string will be converted by means of the transformational rule $B + D + E \rightarrow E + B$ into the string $c + g + h + a + d + e$ with the associated phrase marker shown in Figure 4. In other words, since the string of terminal symbols itself constitutes part of the phrase marker, we can say that the rule converts one phrase marker into another; and this is the defining property of transformational rules. The rule I have just given has the effect of deleting everything dominated by D (including D itself) and permuting B and E, keeping their internal structure intact. The phrase marker given in Figure 3 and the phrase marker given in Figure 4 may be described, respectively, as *underlying* and *derived*, with respect to the transformation in question. (In deciding that the derived phrase marker has the particular form I have attributed to it in Figure 4, I have begged an important theoretical question, to which we will return briefly in a moment.)

If we now look at our illustrative underlying string (*the + man + Present + may + have + en + open + the + door*) and at the associated phrase marker (which I have left the reader to construct for himself),

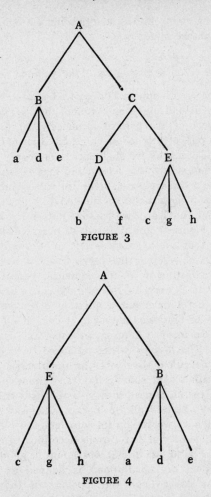

FIGURE 3

FIGURE 4

we shall see that *the + man* is wholly dominated by
NP, Present + may + have + en by *Aux*, the single
element *open* by *V*; and *the + door* by *NP*. This
means that transformational Rule 13 is applicable and,
if applied (for it is an optional rule), will convert the

underlying string into Rule 13a with the appropriate derived phrase marker:

(13a) *the + door + Present + may + have + en +*
 be + en + open + by + the + man

But what is the appropriate derived phrase marker? This is a difficult question. Granted that NP_2 becomes the subject of the passive sentence, that *be + en* becomes part of *Aux* in the same way that *have + en* or *may* is (this, as we shall see, is necessary for the operation of subsequent rules), and that *by* is attached to NP_1 to form a phrase, there are still a number of points about the structure of the derived phrase marker that remain unclear. Two possible phrase markers are given in Figures 5 and 6. It will be observed that they differ in that one takes *by + NP_1* to be a part of the verb phrase, whereas the other treats it as an immediate constituent of the sentence, equivalent in "status," as it were, to NP_2 and *VP*. (It will also be noticed that I have put a question mark where the label for the bracketed phrase *by + NP_1* should be.)

We have touched here on an important theoretical problem. The derived string produced by one transformational rule may serve as the underlying string for the operation of a subsequent transformational rule, and will therefore need to have associated with it the appropriate derived phrase marker. Chomsky and his followers have worked on this problem and have tried to establish a set of conventions according to which a particular kind of formal operation (e.g., deletion, permutation, or substitution) is defined to have a particular effect upon the topology of the phrase marker it transforms; and we followed these conventions when we decided that the effect of the rule $B + D + E \rightarrow E + B$, operating upon the underlying phrase marker shown in Figure 3, was the derived phrase marker in Figure 4. But this was a very simple example from the point of view of the operations in-

FIGURE 5

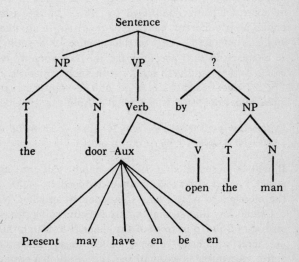

FIGURE 6

volved and the shape of the phrase marker to which
they applied, and furthermore it was a purely abstract
example unaffected by any empirical considerations.
The reader will appreciate that the situation is very
different when it comes to formulating a set of transformational rules for the description of English or some
other natural language.

I shall now introduce, and briefly discuss, two
further transformational rules (slightly different in
form from the corresponding rules in *Syntactic Structures*, but based upon them and having the same
general effect). The first is the obligatory "number
transformation":

$$(14) \quad Present \rightarrow \begin{cases} s \ / \ NP_{sing} \text{ ——} \\ o \ / \text{ elsewhere} \end{cases}$$

This is a context-sensitive rule, which says that *Present*
is to be rewritten as *s* if and only if it is immediately
preceded in the underlying string by a sequence of one
or more elements dominated by NP_{sing} in the associated phrase marker, but is to be rewritten in all other
contexts as "zero" (i.e., as the absence of a suffix).
It is this rule that accounts for the "agreement" between subject and verb manifest in such sentences as
The man goes vs. **The man go*, or *The man is . . .* vs.
*The man are . . . . If it is applied to Rule 13a it yields:

(14a) the + door + s + may + have + en + be +
      en + open + by + the + man

It will be observed that what we might call the "abstract" verbal suffix *s* is here introduced *in front of*
the element to which it is subsequently attached (in
the same way that *en* and *ing* are introduced by phrase
structure Rule 10 in front of the element to which they
are later attached). I have called these "abstract"
suffixes because, as we shall see, they assume a variety
of forms, including "zero" in various contexts.

The rule by which these "abstract" suffixes are placed after the appropriate stems (the "auxiliary transformation") may be given as follows:

$$(15) \begin{Bmatrix} Tense \\ en \\ ing \end{Bmatrix} + \begin{Bmatrix} M \\ have \\ be \\ V \end{Bmatrix} \rightarrow \begin{Bmatrix} M \\ have \\ be \\ V \end{Bmatrix} + \begin{Bmatrix} Tense \\ en \\ ing \end{Bmatrix}$$

This rule says that any pair of elements the first of which is *Tense*, *en*, or *ing*, and the second of which is M, *have*, *be*, or V, are to be (obligatorily) permuted, the rest of the string to the left and the rest of the string to the right remaining unchanged. If the rule is applied to 14a it will permute *s* + *may* (i.e., *Tense* + M), *en* + *be*, and *en* + *open* (*en* + V) successively from left to right, yielding:

(15a) *the* + *door* + *may* + *s* + *have* + *be* + *en* + *open* + *en* + *by* + *the* + *man*

One more transformational rule has yet to apply, which puts a word-boundary symbol (I shall use a space) between every pair of elements the second of which is not *Tense*, *en*, or *ing* and the first of which is not M, *have*, *be*, or V. Applied to Rule 15a, this yields:

(16a) *the door may* + *s have be* + *en open* + *en by the man*

And this is the form that our illustrative string would have after all the relevant transformational rules have operated.

Finally, in a grammar of the kind outlined by Chomsky in *Syntactic Structures*, there is a set of "morphophonemic" rules, which will convert the string of words and morphemes into a string of phonemes.

These would rewrite *may + s* as the phonemic representation of what is spelled *may*, *open + en* as what is spelled *opened*, (*be + s* as what is spelled *is*, *run + en* as what is spelled *run*, and so on). We end up, therefore, as we should, with the phonemic representation of *The door may have been opened by the man.*

Those readers who were previously unfamiliar with Chomsky's system of transformational grammar may have found it rather tedious working through this step-by-step derivation of a single sentence. But they will now have acquired a sufficient understanding of the way the grammar is designed and operates for them to appreciate the significance of some of the more general points made in this and later chapters. At this stage in our discussion of transformational grammar, it may be helpful to introduce a diagram showing how the grammar outlined in *Syntactic Structures* was organized. (See Figure 7.) The input to the grammar is the initial

FIGURE 7

element (as explained in the previous chapter), which generates a set of underlying strings by means of the phrase structure rules in the first "box" of the diagram. The second "box" comprises the transformational rules, of which some are optional and others obligatory. These rules take as their "input" single underlying strings, or pairs of underlying strings (we shall come back to this point), and by successively modifying these strings and their associated phrase markers, generate as their "output" all and only the sentences of the language, represented as strings of words and morphemes, and assign to each sentence its derived constituent structure. The third "box" of rules then converts each of these sentences from its syntactic representation as a string of words and morphemes to its phonological representation as a string of phonemes (and in this way relates the two levels of analysis that were referred to in Chapter ii by means of the term "duality" of structure).

According to this model of generative grammar, different types of simple sentences are accounted for by means of *optional* transformational rules. For example, all the following sentences are related in that they derive from the same underlying string:

(1) *The man opened the door.*
(2) *The man did not open the door.*
(3) *Did the man open the door?*
(4) *Didn't the man open the door?*
(5) *The door was opened by the man.*
(6) *The door was not opened by the man.*
(7) *Was the door opened by the man?*
(8) *Wasn't the door opened by the man?*

They differ in that: (1) has had no optional transformation applied to the underlying string; (2) has had the *Negative* transformation applied; (3) the *Interrogative*; (4) the *Negative* and *Interrogative*; (5) the *Passive*; (6) the *Passive* and *Negative*; (7) the *Passive* and *Interrogative*; and (8) the *Passive*, *Negative*, and *Interrogative*. Of these eight sentences, the first (a simple, active, declarative sentence) is defined by Chomsky, in *Syntactic Structures*, as a *kernel sentence*. It should be emphasized (and this is clear from our detailed consideration of the derivative of a passive sentence above) that nonkernel sentences, such as (2) and (8), are not derived from kernel sentences, such as (1), but from a common underlying string. That is to say, there are no sentences generated without the application of at least a small number of *obligatory* transformations, including rules comparable in effect with Rules 14 and 15 above.

Compound sentences, in which two clauses are *co-ordinated* (e.g., *The man opened the door and switched on the light*), and complex sentences, in which one clause is *subordinated* to another (e.g., *The man who opened the door switched on the light*), are generated by means of *conjoining* and *embedding* transformations, respectively, which take as "input" a pair of underlying strings (e.g., *the + man + Past + open + the + door +* and *the + man + Past + switch + on + the + light*) and combine them in various ways. Conjoining and embedding transformations constitute the class of *generalized* transformations in *Syntactic Structures*; and it is the repeated application of these rules that accounts for the existence of such recursive structures as *This is the . . . that lived in the house that Jack built*, or *a big, black, three-foot-long, . . . , wooden box* (see pages 42–43). All the generalized transformations are, of course, optional.

So much, then, by way of a general summary of the earlier version of transformational grammar presented in *Syntactic Structures*. Chomsky claimed that one of the advantages of this system, the third and most powerful of his "models for the description of language," was that it could account more satisfactorily than phrase structure grammar for certain types of structural ambiguity. To take one of Chomsky's famous examples: A sentence like *Flying planes can be dangerous* is ambiguous (cf., *To fly planes can be dangerous* and *Planes that are flying can be dangerous*); and yet, under both interpretations, the immediate constituent analysis is, presumably, (((*flying*) (*planes*)) (((*can*) (*be*)) (*dangerous*))). This is a different kind of structural ambiguity from that manifest in a phrase like *old men and women* discussed in the previous chapter. It would be possible to generate a sentence like *Flying planes can be dangerous* within a phrase structure grammar and to assign to it two different phrase markers—differing with respect to the labels assigned to the node dominating *flying*. But this would not be an intuitively satisfying account of the ambiguity; and it would fail to relate to the phrase *flying planes*, on the one hand, to *planes that are flying*, and, on the other, to *someone flies planes*. The transformational analysis accounts for the ambiguity by relating two different underlying strings (let us say, *plane + s + be + ing + fly* and *someone + fly + plane + s*) to the same derived string. Many other examples could be given of structurally ambiguous sentences that can be accounted for rather nicely in terms of transformational grammar: *I don't like eating apples* (i.e., *apples for eating* vs. *to eat apples*), *I disapprove of his drinking* (i.e., *the fact that he drinks* vs. *the way in which he drinks*), etc.[2]

This transformational explanation of structural ambiguity depends upon the application of *optional* rules, and it is in accord with the more general principle (which may be taken as axiomatic in the study of any system of communication) that meaning implies *choice*. This principle, it should be observed, states that the possibility of selecting one alternative rather than another is a *necessary*, but not a *sufficient*, condition for the expression of a difference of meaning. The most obvious application of the principle is when one word rather than another is selected from the set of words that could occur in a given position (cf., *The man opened the windows* vs. *The man opened the door*). Here we are concerned with the "choice" of a different set of rules (or a difference in the order in which the same set of rules is applied) in the generation of two or more sentences from the same underlying string. I have said that "choice," in this sense, is not a *sufficient* condition for there being a difference of

2 Cf., Chomsky, *Language and Mind*, p. 27.

meaning in the resultant sentences. For example, *John looked the word up in the dictionary* and *John looked up the word in the dictionary* differ (according to *Syntactic Structures*) in that an additional optional transformation has been applied in the generation of the former sentence. The two sentences are not, however, different in meaning; and the transformational rule in question (which has the effect of converting *Past + look + up + the + word* to *Past + look + the +word + up* at a particular point in the derivation) may be described as *stylistic*.

In 1965, in *Aspects of the Theory of Syntax*, Chomsky put forward a more comprehensive theory of transformational grammar, which differed from the earlier theory in a number of important respects. For our purposes, it will be sufficient to mention only the most general· differences between the *Syntactic Structures* grammar and what we may .call an *Aspects*-type grammar. Once again, a diagram may be helpful.

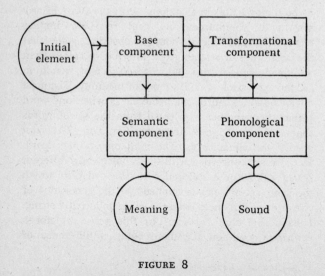

FIGURE 8

The most striking difference between the two grammars, as represented in Figures 7 and 8, is the additional "box" of rules in the *Aspects*-type grammar labeled "Semantic component." In *Syntactic Structures* it was argued that, although semantic considerations are not directly relevant to the syntactic description of sentences, there are "striking correspondences between the structures and elements that are discovered in formal, grammatical analysis and specific semantic functions," and that, "having determined the syntactic structure of the language, we can study the way in which this syntactic structure is put to use in the actual functioning of the language."[3] In the years that followed the publication of *Syntactic Structures*, Chomsky and his collaborators came to the conclusion that the meaning of sentences could, and should, be submitted to the same kind of precise, formal analysis as their syntactic structure, and that semantics should be included as an integral part of the grammatical analysis of languages. The grammar of a language is now seen by Chomsky as a system of rules relating the meaning (or meanings) of each sentence it generates to the physical manifestation of the sentences in the medium of sound.

In *Aspects*, as in *Syntactic Structures*, the syntax falls into two parts. But the two syntactic components operate somewhat differently. It is now the *base* of the grammar (which is roughly comparable with the phrase structure part of the earlier system), rather than the transformational component, that accounts for the semantically relevant options, including the possibility of forming recursive constructions. The difference between a declarative and an interrogative sentence, or between an active and a passive sentence, is no longer described in terms of optional transformations, but in terms of a choice made in the base rules.

[3] *Syntactic Structures*, pp. 101, 102.

For example, there might be a base rule of the following form:

(2a) $VP \rightarrow Verb + NP \; (+ Agentive)$

and the selection of the element *Agentive* would distinguish the strings underlying passive sentences from the strings underlying the corresponding active sentences. There would then be an *obligatory* transformational rule, corresponding to Rule 13 (page 63), operating if and only if the "input" string contained the element *Agentive*. This proposal (which corresponds with Chomsky's in spirit, rather than in detail) has the advantage that, if we formulate the transformational rule correctly, it gives us a label for the node dominating $by + NP_1$ in the derived phrase markers associated with passive sentences (page 66).

The base rules generate an indefinitely large set of underlying phrase markers (which represent the *deep structure* of all the sentences characterized by the system), and these are converted into derived phrase markers (which represent the *surface structure* of the sentences) by the transformational rules, most of which (apart from "stylistic" rules) are now obligatory. The meaning of each sentence is derived, mainly if not wholly, from its deep structure, by means of the rules of semantic interpretation; and the phonetic interpretation of each sentence—its physical description as an acoustic "signal"—is derived from its surface structure by means of the phonological rules.

We need not go into the more technical details that distinguish an *Aspects*-type grammar from the conceptually simpler system of *Syntactic Structures*. All that remains to be added to this account of the general characteristics of the 1965 version of transformational grammar is that various semantically relevant grammatical notions are now explicitly defined in terms of deep structure relations. (This was merely hinted at in

Syntactic Structures.) We may note, in particular, the distinction between the "logical" (deep structure) and "grammatical" (surface structure) subject of a sentence. The "logical" subject is the *NP* that is immediately dominated by *S* (= *Sentence*) in the deep structure; the "grammatical" subject is the leftmost *NP*, which is immediately dominated by (the topmost) *S* in the surface structure. For example, in the sentence *John was persuaded by Harry to take up golf*, the grammatical subject is *John* (it is this notion of "subject" that is relevant to the statement of the agreement holding between the subject and the verb in English: *John was persuaded* vs. *They were persuaded*, etc.). But the deep structure of this sentence consists of one sentence (S_2) embedded within another (S_1), and each sentence has its own logical subject. We can represent the deep structure of this sentence, informally and omitting all but the essential information, as it is given in Figure 9. It will be seen that the logical subject of S_1 (the *matrix* sentence) is *Harry*, and that

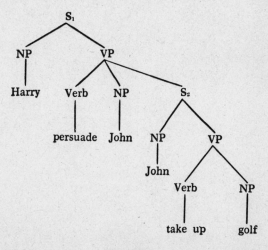

FIGURE 9

of S_2 (the *embedded* sentence) is *John*. Furthermore, the deep structure subject of S_2 is identical with the deep structure object of S_1 (the *NP* that is immediately dominated by *VP*). As Chomsky points out, it is these deep structure relations that are essential for the correct semantic interpretation of the sentence.

Recent Developments in Chomskyan
and Post-Chomskyan Linguistics

• • •
viii

In this chapter, we shall look at some of the developments that have taken place in linguistics since 1965, when, as we have just seen, Chomsky put forward a far more comprehensive theory of transformational grammar than he did in his earlier work. Chomsky himself now refers to his 1965 theory as the *standard theory* of transformational grammar. We will use the same term, although it has been thought by some of Chomsky's critics to be unfairly loaded in favor of the system of transformational grammar outlined in *Aspects of the Theory of Syntax*.

The standard theory of *Aspects* is to be contrasted, on the one hand, with Chomsky's own *extended standard theory* and, on the other, with what may be regarded, from Chomsky's point of view at least, as nonstandard theories—of which there are now an almost bewildering variety competing for acceptance. Many of these might also be described from a more neutral vantage point as extensions of the standard theory. To avoid confusion, however, we will reserve the term "extended standard theory" for Chomsky's own modifications of the 1965 version of transformational grammar. Before we embark upon the task of comparing the best-known and more important of the nonstandard theories with the standard theory, and subsequently with Chomsky's extended standard theory, I must explain what I mean by "Chomskyan" and "post-Chomskyan" in the title of this chapter. It might well be objected that these terms are as misleading in their way as "standard" and "extended standard" are.

As I pointed out in the Introduction, the "Chomskyan" school of linguistics is not just one among many. If it was true when the first edition of this book was published, in 1970, it is even more obviously the case now (in 1977) that every school of linguistics tends to define its position on major theoretical issues in relation to Chomsky's pronouncements on the same issues. There is a sense, therefore, in which all the theories that we are going to consider are Chomskyan —and it is for this reason that we are concerned with them here. Some of them, however, are also post-Chomskyan in the rather special sense that they are deliberately presented by their authors as replacing, or supplanting, the standard theory of transformational grammar. Of course, the extended standard theory might also be described as post-Chomskyan in this sense, but I shall reserve the term "Chomskyan" for developments in the theory of transformational grammar initiated or approved by Chomsky himself. It is an indication of Chomsky's stature in the field that so much of what is intended to be post-Chomskyan—an antithesis to one or another of his theses—should also be, in other respects, very obviously Chomskyan. Indeed the history of the past ten years can be summed up, as far as Chomskyan and post-Chomskyan developments are concerned, as thesis, antithesis—and counterthesis!—but so far no synthesis!

The most immediate distinctively post-Chomskyan challenge to the standard theory has come from *case grammar*. As we saw at the end of the preceding chapter, Chomsky drew a distinction in *Aspects* between the deep structure subject or object and the surface structure subject or object of a sentence and claimed that it was the deep structure functions that were semantically relevant. Many linguists, however, have taken the view that notions like "subject" and "object" are relatively superficial, that their definitions vary from language to language, and that they play no part in determining the meaning of the sentence as such. In an influential paper published in 1968, "The Case for Case," C. J. Fillmore argued that the most satisfactory grammatical analysis of a sentence was one in which the constituents of each clause, at the deepest level of syntactic analysis, were what he called *cases*, for example, agent, instrument, and place.

This use of the term "case" is a generalization of the more traditional usage, according to which, in certain languages, different forms of the same noun are said to differ in case (nominative, accusative, genitive, dative, and so on) and verbs (and prepositions) are said to govern their objects, or complements, in such and such a case. For example, in Latin the object of the verb *videre* ("to see") must be in the accusative case (e.g., *hominem*: "a/the man"); the object of *meminisse* ("to remember"), in the genitive (e.g., *hominis*: "a/the man"); the object of *imperare* ("to order"), in the dative (e.g., *homini*: "a/the man"); and so on. The subject of all these verbs, as generally in Latin, is in the nominative (e.g., *homo*: "a/the man"); and the subject is not traditionally regarded as being governed by the verb in the way that the object is. In Latin, as in many languages (such as Russian and German), nouns are inflected for case:

homo, hominem, hominis, and *homini* are all forms of
the same noun (conventionally referred to by means
of the nominative form, *homo*). In English (as in
French, Italian, or Spanish—not to mention Chinese,
Malay, and a vast number of other languages) nouns
are not inflected for case, such inflectional variation
as there is in English being restricted to pronouns:
Cf., *he* vs. *him*, *I* vs. *me*, *they* vs. *them*, etc. From a
more general point of view, however, prepositions or
postpositions can be thought of as having the same
kind of semantic and syntactic function as the cases
have in a case-inflected language. (The difference
between prepositions, e.g., *to*, *by*, or *from* in English,
and postpositions is that, whereas prepositions come
before the noun phrase with which they are associated,
postpositions come after. Many languages, such as
Turkish, Japanese, and Hindi, have postpositions. For
convenience, I shall use the more familiar term
"preposition" in what follows, to cover both prepositions and postpositions.)

Up to a point, it is possible to assign particular
meanings to what would be traditionally called cases
in the grammatical analysis of languages like Latin—
meanings having to do with agency, location, the
source or goal of movement, and the like—and, in
terms of these meanings, to put the case-inflected noun
phrases (with or without prepositions) of Latin and
other such languages into functional correspondence
with noun phrases and adverbial phrases in languages
that do not have case in the traditional sense of the
term. Indeed, it has long been common practice to
make use of the notions of agency, location, and the
source or goal of movement in the grammatical analysis of languages of strikingly different grammatical
structure. What is distinctive about *case grammar*
(although it has its precursors, in pre-Chomskyan
linguistics, in the work of scholars such as Hjelmslev
and, especially, Tesnière) is the identification of case

as a deep structure category. There are several versions of case grammar, of which Fillmore's is the best known.

In case grammar, the verb occupies a central, or pivotal, position in the sentence; and each verb governs (in a recognizably extended sense of this traditional term) a set of obligatory and/or optional deep structure cases, which are filled, as it were, by expressions that may occur as subjects, objects, or prepositional phrases at a more superficial level. For example, the verb *open* might be classified in the lexicon associated with a case grammar of English as one that governs an agent, an entity, and, optionally, an instrument. (The term "entity" is not Fillmore's; it refers to the most neutral, semantically undifferentiated, deep structure case, which is labeled differently by different authors.) Such sentences as (1) *The jailer opened the door (with a key)*, (2) *The door was opened (by the jailer) (with a key)*, (3) *The door opened*, (4) *The key opened the door*, and the like would all be derived, in Fillmore's version of case grammar, from an underlying structure in which *(by) the jailer* has the case role of agent, *the door* has the case role of entity, and *(with) the key* has the case role of instrument. The agent expression (the expression that is in the agent case or has the case role of agent in the deep structure specification) is the subject in (1) but an omissible adverbial modifier in (2)—cf., Figures 5 and 6 and Rule (13) of Chapter vii; the entity expression is the object in (1) but the subject in (2); the instrument expression is an omissible adverbial modifier in (1) and (2) but the subject in (4). Sentences (1)–(4), and others, are transformationally related in case grammar by virtue of their being derived from common deep structure (due allowance being made for the distinction of obligatory and optional cases).

It is not difficult to see the attractions of case grammar. Notions having to do with agency and causation, location and locomotion, acting on behalf of or to the advantage (or disadvantage) of someone, and similar notions that have been involved in works on case grammar, are of more obvious semantic relevance than the grammatical relations associated with the distinction between subject and predicate or subject and object; they are readily identifiable across languages (in at least the most typical situations in which each such notion is invoked); and they have been recognized by a number of psychologists as playing an important part in the acquisition of language by children. Despite these attractions, case grammar is no longer seen by the majority of linguists working within the general framework of transformational-generative grammar as a viable alternative to the standard theory. The reason is that, when it comes to classifying the totality of the verbs in a language in terms of the deep structure cases they govern, the semantic criteria that define these cases are all too often unclear or in conflict.

Neither Chomsky nor any of his followers has been paying much attention recently to case grammar as such. But Fillmore's "Case for Case" has had its effect on the development of the extended standard theory. Chomsky now attaches more importance than he did in *Aspects* to what he, rather misleadingly, refers to, in his most recent publications, as "thematic relations"—misleadingly because the terms "theme" and "thematic" are well established in linguistics in a quite different sense (and one that is closer to their everyday, nontechnical sense). But Fillmore's version of case grammar, although it is the best known and so far the most influential, is but one version of what may be more generally, and more satisfactorily, described as *valency grammar*; and it would be unwise to rule out the possibility of some kind of valency grammar's being developed as a successful rival to the standard and extended standard theories.

Valency grammars are normally formalized (insofar as they have been formalized) as *dependency grammars*, which (like *categorial grammars*) are weakly, and perhaps strongly, equivalent to phrase structure grammars. (See Appendix 1.) They directly reflect the view that within the sentence (or its propositional nucleus) there is a single governing element—the verb—and a set of dependent expressions whose number and semantic, or logical, type is determined by the *valency* of the verb. This notion of valency (the term "valency" having been borrowed from chemistry) was introduced into linguistics by the French scholar Tesnière, whose work lacked the mathematical precision of that of Chomsky or Harris but can be seen in certain respects as foreshadowing the development of transformational grammar. The notion of valency clearly derives from, but extends, the traditional distinction of transitive and intransitive verbs; and it can be related to the classification of predicates, in formal logic, in terms of the number of expressions with which they can be combined in well-formed formulas. It is undoubtedly true, for many languages at least, that the selection of a particular verb determines to a considerable degree the grammatical structure of the sentence (or its propositional nucleus). So far the notion of valency has been more extensively discussed and applied in Germany and the Soviet Union than elsewhere, but certain of the central ideas of valency grammar are also to be found in some of the more obviously post-Chomskyan work that is now being published.

For example, one of the most recent developments in post-Chomskyan syntax is the emergence of what its adherents call relational grammar. Unlike some of the other proposed alternatives to the standard theory, relational grammar attaches considerable importance to the grammatical relations of being subject, object, or indirect object of the sentence. It operates (as

Tesnière did) with a hierarchical ordering of subject, object, and indirect object; and it uses this hierarchical ordering to determine what position in a phrase marker will be occupied by which expression when one phrase marker is converted into another by means of a transformational rule. In this respect, relational grammar can claim to be more traditional than the standard theory is, for good or ill, in the way in which it establishes a transformational correspondence between active and passive sentences. The effect of switching from the active to the passive is to reduce the valency of the verb by eliminating the subject expression or demoting it to the status of an optional, and structurally dispensable, part of the propositional nucleus. But in English, and many other languages, every sentence must have a grammatical subject. So— to make the point informally and in deliberately traditional terms—the object of the active becomes the subject of the passive. The converse process is seen, in many languages, in the formation of causative constructions, for example, in the formation of a sentence meaning *John got Bill to kill Harry* from the structure underlying a sentence meaning *Bill killed Harry*. Here the valency of the two-place (that is, transitive) verb meaning *kill* is augmented. The resultant three-place causative verb meaning *cause to kill* takes as its subject not the subject or object of the inner transitive verb but the additional expression referring, characteristically, to the causal agent; and this, in many languages, involves the demotion of the subject of the inner verb to the status of indirect object in the three-place structure (the position of direct object being filled already). It is important not to exaggerate the similarities between valency grammar and relational grammar—the more so because relational grammar has not yet been widely exemplified in the published literature—but there are certain discernible similarities of the kind mentioned in this paragraph.

What is generally regarded as a more serious challenge to the standard theory comes from *generative semantics*. Though it is now firmly entrenched in current discussions of linguistic theory, the term "generative semantics" is misleading in several respects. Generative semantics is not merely, or even primarily, a theory of semantics. Still less is "generative" in contrast with "nongenerative," in this context, as it is when one talks about the difference between generative grammar and pre-Chomskyan, nongenerative grammar. The term "generative semantics" refers to an alternative version of transformational-generative grammar—one that differs from the standard version of *Aspects* in that the rules of the semantic component are said to be "generative" rather than "interpretive."

According to the standard theory, every sentence has two identifiable levels of syntactic structure: *deep structure* and *surface structure*. Deep structures are phrase markers (containing lexical items) that are generated by the rules of the base component. They are converted into surface structures by the application of an ordered set of transformational rules, some of which apply cyclically. (See Appendix 1.) The deep structures serve as input to the semantic component; and the surface structures, as input to the phonological component. (See Figure 8.) Both the semantic rules and the phonological rules are purely *interpretive*: The function of the semantic rules is to interpret the output of the base component by assigning to each sentence a *semantic representation* (or several semantic representations in the case of ambiguous sentences) as the function of the phonological rules is to assign to each sentence a phonetic representation. The term "interpret," it should be noted, is here being used in a technical sense. The semantic interpretation associated with a sentence by the grammar is not its meaning but a formal representation of its meaning (in what is, strictly speaking, a formal metalanguage—see Ap-

pendix 1) in terms of a set of symbols each of which
denotes a universal atomic concept, and the phonetic
interpretation of a sentence is not its pronunciation
but a formal representation of its pronunciation in
terms of a set of symbols each of which denotes some
universal phonetic feature. These symbols are the elements, or *primes*, of the semantic and the phonetic
levels of representation, respectively; and the notion
"level of representation" is rigorously defined within
Chomsky's formalization of the theory of grammar.
(See Appendix 1.)

But the standard theory is formulated within the
framework of certain more general Chomskyan beliefs
about the nature of language and linguistic competence. In particular, it is Chomsky's belief that every
speaker of any natural language (by virtue of his
possession of the specifically human capacity to acquire
language) knows, in some sense, what counts as a
humanly possible speech sound and what counts as a
humanly possible concept (or conceptual distinction),
and that he also knows some of the conditions that
determine the well-formed combinations of sounds and
meanings that are brought together in the words and
sentences of particular languages. We will come back
to this part of Chomsky's thought in Chapters ix and x.
It suffices for the present to emphasize the fact that,
when Chomsky says that the grammar of a particular
language (a language-particular grammar) is a system
of rules and principles that link sound with meaning,
he is taking for granted the native speaker's ability
to perform another kind of interpretation, by means of
which the phonetic representations are converted into
sound and the phonetic representations into meaning.
The missing links are supplied, in intent at least, by
the more general theory of grammar, which Chomsky
refers to as *universal grammar*. It is by virtue of his
knowledge of universal grammar that the speaker of
a natural language is held to be able to interpret the

phonetic and semantic representations (or, more precisely, the mental schemata that are their psychological correlates in language performance).

Generative semantics is far from being as radical an alternative to the standard theory as it has sometimes seemed to be both to its proponents and to some of its opponents. Like Chomsky, the generative semanticists take the view that language-particular grammars are generative devices whose function it is to relate semantic representations and phonetic representations; they operate with the same kind of semantic and phonetic primes; they make essentially the same assumptions as Chomsky does about the native speaker's ability to interpret these primes (or their cognitive correlates) by virtue of his knowledge of universal grammar; and, finally, the kind of grammatical model to which they appeal is not merely generative but transformational. What, then, is the difference between generative semantics and the standard theory?

At first sight, the difference is clear enough: The standard-theory model is syntactically based, and the generative-semantics model is semantically based. That is to say, whereas the standard theory puts all the generative capacity of the grammar in the syntax (and more particularly in the base component), generative semantics puts all the generative capacity of the grammar in the rules of semantic well-formedness. It is this conception of the difference between generative semantics and the standard theory that accounts for the use of the term "generative semantics" in the first place. But now, after some years of involved and at times acrimonious argument, it is accepted by both the proponents and the opponents of generative semantics that its difference from the standard theory cannot be characterized simply in terms of the directionality of the relation that holds between syntax and semantics. Much of the initial plausibility of generative semantics disappears when this point is appreciated. It is only too easy to think of a generative grammar as a model of the language user's production and comprehension of actual utterances. (Cf., Chapter iv.) Looked at from this point of view, the generative-semantics model can be seen as the one that more directly reflects the conversion of meaning to sound in production and of sound to meaning in comprehension. But neither the standard-theory model nor the generative-semantics model is intended to be a model of language performance. Furthermore, it is hardly more realistic to think of the production of utterances as a process in which the speaker first of all forms in his mind a sentence-sized idea, as it were, and only then selects a syntactic structure and words with which to express this idea than it is to conceive of it as a process in which the speaker first decides on some syntactic structure and then chooses words to fit it. What then is the difference between the standard theory and generative semantics when they are both regarded as models of competence rather than performance?

The principal difference is that, whereas the standard theory draws a distinction between the deep structure of a sentence and its semantic interpretation (the latter being derived from the former by the purely interpretive projection rules of the semantic component), the generative-semantics theory draws no such distinction. According to the generative-semantics hypothesis, the deep structure of a sentence is its semantic representation; and this is converted into a surface structure, in much the same way as an *Aspects*-type deep structure is converted into a surface structure, by means of the application, in sequence, of a set of transformational rules. Since Chomskyan transformational rules, by definition, convert phrase markers into phrase markers, it follows that, for the generative semanticist, the semantic representation of a sentence is a phrase marker (a labeled bracketing). However, it differs from an *Aspects*-type deep structure (which, as we have seen, is also a labeled bracketing) in that its terminal elements are not words, like *kill* or *man* in English, but semantic primes like CAUSE, COME ABOUT, NOT, and EXISTENT or MALE, ADULT, and HUMAN.

The generative semanticists have justified their rejection of an independent, syntactically motivated level of deep structure by observing that pairs of sentences that differ in terms of their syntactic structure and the words that they contain may be semantically equivalent (or at least semantically related to each other) in much the same way as pairs of sentences that are held to be transformationally related in an *Aspects*-type grammar: Cf., *John used the key to open the door* and *John opened the door with the key*, or *John bought the car from Harry* and *Harry sold the car to John*. Whether such pairs of sentences have exactly the same meaning or not is debatable, but they will serve our present purpose. Granted that *John bought the car from Harry* and *Harry sold the car to John* are derived from a common underlying semantic representation, the words *sell* and *buy* would be inserted into the phrase markers by a transformational rule of substitution operating upon different syntactically structured complexes of semantic primes. These rules of *lexicalization* (unlike the very different rules of lexicalization in the standard theory) would not apply at a distinct and identifiable level of syntactic representation (the level of deep structure) but would be scattered, as it were, throughout the other transformational rules.

Generative semantics is best regarded, perhaps, as the culmination and consolidation of several tendencies, all of which are present elsewhere in post-Chomskyan linguistics. The most obvious of these is the tendency to motivate syntactic rules by means of semantic evidence. As we saw in Chapter iii, Chomsky took a characteristically "Bloomfieldian" view of the relation between syntax and semantics in his earliest work (without, however, accepting Bloomfield's behavioristic notion of meaning), but it has always been evident, both to Chomsky and to Harris, that (as Harris made the point in 1957) "some major element of meaning remains constant under transformation." By the mid-1960s many linguists (notably J. J. Katz and P. M. Postal, whose work was particularly influential) were prepared to drop the qualification implicit in the phrase "some major element," saying, forcefully and programmatically, "Transformations do not change meaning." This slogan expresses a point of view that Chomsky accepted, at least tentatively, at the time that he was writing *Aspects*. In terms of the standard theory (all the "nonstylistic" transformational rules being obligatory), identity of deep structure is a sufficient condition of identity of meaning. The generative semanticist goes farther: He makes identity of meaning a sufficient condition for postulating transformational relatedness and identity of deep structure. In doing so, he is carrying to an extreme the practice of using semantic data as evidence for syntactic relatedness. But this practice was common in almost all the transformational work, both Chomskyan and post-Chomskyan, that was published in the decade following the appearance of *Aspects*. It is partly a cause and partly a consequence of the greatly increased attention that linguists have been paying to semantics in recent years.

Another general tendency of much post-Chomskyan linguistics is the acceptance of a point of view that can be summed up in the slogans "Deep structures are universal" and "All languages have the same deep structure." The second of these is, strictly speaking, uninterpretable in terms of the Chomskyan notion of deep structure: Languages do not have a deep structure (or a surface structure), but each sentence of a language does. Translated into Chomskyan terms, the second slogan (which is not uncommon, in the form in which I have just given it, in the nonlinguistic literature) might read as follows: "All natural languages have (that is, are generated by) the same base component (excluding the lexicon)." Interpreted in this way, the second slogan expresses what has come to be called the universal base hypothesis, and more will be said about this presently. Neither the generative-semantics theory nor the standard theory commits its adherents to the universal base hypothesis. (It is worth pointing out, in passing, that Chomsky himself has never subscribed to it, although what he has said about formal and substantive universals has often been misunderstood as implying that he does— see Chapter x.) But many transformational grammarians, from both the "generativist" and the "interpretivist" camps, have been attracted by the universal base hypothesis; and they have seen as evidence for it a kind of convergence in the increasingly "deep" or "abstract" analyses that linguists have been providing for "superficially" dissimilar structures in different languages.

The reader will note that I deliberately slipped into the last sentence the words "deep," "superficial," and "abstract," signaling the fact that I was using them loosely, not to say equivocally, by putting them between quotation marks. It is quite possible to define a notion of transformational depth (in terms of the number of rules applying in the generation of the phrase marker, or otherwise). It is arguable, however, that the universal base hypothesis has gained some of its support from the very looseness with which such evocative, and potentially equivocal, words as "deep," "abstract," and "superficial" have been used in its formulation. However that may be, it is undeniable that it has seemed to be an attractive hypothesis, not just to the generative semanticists but also to many linguists who would disagree with them on other issues.

There is, of course, an important difference between a "generativist" and an "interpretivist" version of the universal base hypothesis. There is no *Aspects*-type base component in a generative-semantics model. Instead, there are formation rules whose function it is to generate a set of well-formed semantic representations. It is the formation rules, therefore, that are held to be universal by the generative semanticist. In contrast, an "interpretist" who subscribes to the universal base hypothesis is committed to the very different (and, at first sight at least, far more interesting) proposition that the purely syntactic rules of an *Aspects*-type base component are universal. We will come back to this point.

A third general tendency of much of the most recent Chomskyan and post-Chomskyan linguistics is the ever increasing employment of the conceptual and terminological apparatus of modern formal logic and formal semantics. Both "generativists" and "interpretivists" have concentrated their attention, in the last few years, on a range of topics (negation, quantification, presupposition, and so on) whose clarification and analysis owe much to the work of logicians and philosophers. Generative semanticists, in particular, have been inclined to identify the deep structure of a sentence (that is, its semantic representation) with what a philosopher would refer to as its *logical form*. For example, a sentence like *Everyone loves someone* is ambiguous with respect to its logical form; and its ambiguity is accounted for, in standard systems of formal logic, by the relative order of the quantifiers (the formal correlates of *everyone* and *someone*) in the formulas that represent the two different propositions expressed by the sentence. The generative semanticist would give exactly the same account of the ambiguity, saying that the sentence in question is derived, by transformational rules, from two different semantic representations, the one having *someone* at a higher level than *everyone* in the underlying phrase marker and the other having *everyone* higher than *someone*. In this respect, the generative semanticist's conception of underlying structure closely matches the philosopher's conception of logical form. Indeed, the semantic representations with which generative semanticists operate are almost identical with the formulas of standard first-order logic.

Reference has just been made to the branch of logic known as formal semantics; and this brings us to the last of the alternatives to the standard theory, other than the Chomskyan extended standard theory, that will be dealt with here. In origin, formal semantics was the study of the semantics of the propositional calculus, the predicate calculus, and other formal languages constructed by logicians. (For some discussion of the grammar of formal languages, see Appendix 1.) Usually, the meaning of a sentence in a formal language is defined as its *truth conditions*, the conditions that must be met in any world, or state of affairs, that the sentence purports to describe in order for the sentence to be true. Many formal languages are such that it is possible to construct a finite or infinite set of complex sentences out of a finite set of simple sentences. If a formal language has this syntactic property together with the more particular semantic property that the meaning of every complex sentence is a function of the meanings of the simple sentences of which the complex sentence is composed, the task of providing a semantic analysis of the language (that is, an interpretation of each sentence in terms of its truth conditions) can be split into two parts: (1) that of assigning an interpretation to each of the simple sentences and (2) that of specifying for every distinct means of combining sentences that the syntactic rules of the language permit the principle, or function (in the mathematical sense), that determines the meaning of the resultant combination. The second of these two parts of the semantic analysis will be facilitated if it is the syntactic structure itself that determines the meaning of the successively more complex combinations of sentences. Several formal languages have been constructed that have this property. But formal languages are under the control of their designers and, within limits, they can be provided with whatever properties their designers think fit to provide them with. What about natural languages?

One scholar who took the view that the semantic structure of natural languages could, and should, be analyzed like the semantic structure of formal languages (under a standard truth-conditional interpretation) was the American logician Richard Montague (who died in 1971). He was not alone in taking this view, and what has come to be called *Montague grammar* appears to have won more support so far than other systems that are strongly influenced by work within the field of formal semantics. There is no need for us to go into the technicalities of Montague grammar. It is sufficient to point out that Montague's system differs not only from the *Aspects*-system but also from all the other Chomskyan and post-Chomskyan alternatives considered in this chapter in several respects. The most important has to do with the close correspondence that Montague establishes between the syntax and the semantics, and he does this by adopting a particular kind of *categorial grammar*. (See Appendix 1.) Another important difference between Montague grammar and other kinds of Chomskyan and post-Chomskyan generative grammar is that, when it comes to excluding certain strings of words as ill-formed, Montague throws much more weight on the semantics than he does on the syntax. This is largely a matter of his pretheoretical attitude toward the notion of grammaticality. But it is arguable, and has been argued, that in *Aspects* Chomsky went too far in the other direction, excluding (by means of the device of *selection restrictions*) sentences that, if they are ill-formed (e.g., *Sincerity admires John*), are semantically, not syntactically, ill-formed. It is too early to say what effect Montague grammar will have on linguistics in the next few years. It has been mentioned here because it has a number of powerful advocates among linguists. Although Montague grammar is not strongly influenced by the work of Chomsky, as far as Montague's own development of the system is concerned, it has been suggested recently (notably by Barbara H. Partee) that a more powerful type of Montague grammar could be constructed—a grammar with a categorial base component and a transformational extension to it—and that a Montague grammar of this kind would be more appropriate than any currently available alternative version of transformational grammar, for relating the semantic interpretations of natural-language sentences to their syntactic structure.

Having looked at the most important post-Chomskyan alternatives to the standard theory, we may turn now to the so-called *extended standard theory* of Chomsky and his immediate associates. The extended standard theory has been in a state of more or less continuous development for the past ten years. It differs from generative semantics in that, like the standard theory of *Aspects*, it is an "interpretivist" theory, within which sentences are assigned a deep structure representation distinct from their semantic representation and the transformational rules apply after the insertion of words from the lexicon in the underlying phrase markers. It differs from the standard theory, however, in that it has abandoned the principle that only the deep structure of a sentence is relevant to the determination of its semantic representation. Indeed, the development of the extended standard theory from its earliest version of 1970 (in Chomsky's essay "Deep Structure, Surface Structure and Semantic Interpretation") to its 1976 version (*Reflections on Language*) can be described, in a very general way, as the progressive devaluation, for the process of semantic interpretation, of the notion of deep structure. In the earlier version, the semantic interpretation of a sentence (in the specialized Chomskyan sense of "interpretation") is determined jointly by its deep structure and its surface structure; but more recently Chomsky has come to believe that "a suitably enriched notion of surface structure suffices to determine the meaning of sentences under interpretive rules" (*Reflections on Language*, Chapter 3). What this enrichment of the notion of surface structure consists of is something that cannot be discussed here. It is sufficient for our purposes that it should be seen as involving what I have referred to as a corresponding devaluation of the notion of deep structure.

It is important to realize, however, that, as far as Chomsky is concerned, the notion of deep structure still plays much the same role in syntax as it always has done in his formalization of transformational grammar. (In saying this, I am deliberately glossing over the fact that, for technical reasons, complex sentences did not have unitary deep structures in the 1957 version of transformational grammar. For present purposes at least, the term "deep structure" can be taken to cover, retrospectively, the underlying phrase markers of *Syntactic Structures*. One of the few innovations in the *Aspects* system that can be described, without reservation, as an improvement is the introduction of the notion of generalized phrase markers. Another is the strict separation of the syntax and the lexicon, together with a technique for cross-classifying words in terms of sets of syntactic properties.) In the passage from which the quotation in the previous paragraph was drawn, Chomsky makes it quite clear that the notion of deep structures is, in principle, no more closely bound up with the principle of semantic interpretation than the notion of surface structure is.

He also insists—and this is a very important point for anyone who wishes to understand Chomsky's thought—that there is no correlation between depth, in the technical sense of being transformationally less complex, and either universality or importance: "There is a widespread feeling that semantics is that part of language that is really deep and important, and that the study of language is interesting primarily insofar as it contributes to some understanding of these questions of real profundity." He allows that "there is some merit to this view," but, comparing physics with linguistics and, within linguistics, comparing semantics with phonology, he argues that "physics is significant, applications aside, because of its intellectual depth, and if it were to turn out that the principles of phonology are considerably more sophisticated and intricate than those of semantics, that they enter into nontrivial arguments to explain surprising facts, that they give us much more insight into the nature of the organism, then phonology will be a far deeper theory than semantics, despite the more limited intrinsic interest of the phenomena with which it deals." As we have already seen (and, having pointed this out himself, Chomsky deliberately uses the term "deep" both technically and nontechnically in the passage from which I have just quoted), the several senses in which the word "deep" can be used has led to considerable confusion. This point must be borne constantly in mind when we look at the psychological and philosophical implications of transformational grammar in Chapters ix and x.

We have now almost concluded our general comparative account of the most notable Chomskyan and post-Chomskyan alternatives to the standard theory of 1965. It is no part of my purpose to predict which, if any, of these alternatives will triumph. Nor can there be any question, in a book of this nature, of going into the technical details of the various systems. There is one point of a more technical character, however, that must be made; and this has to do with the relative *power* of different transformational grammars.

As we saw in the preceding three chapters, Chomsky's earliest work in generative grammar was directed toward showing that, of the "three models for the description of language" (to quote the title of his 1956 paper) whose formal properties he had investigated—finite-state grammar, phrase structure grammar, and transformational grammar—the first was definitely not powerful enough for the purpose and the second, though perhaps capable in principle of generating all and only the sentences of any natural language, was not capable of assigning to them structural descriptions that would reveal their formal interrelations. Transformational grammars are intrinsically more powerful than phrase structure grammars. It is arguable, however, that they are too powerful.

The suggestion that the grammar, or a theory, might be condemned on the grounds of its excessive power frequently causes difficulty. The word "powerful," like the word "deep," has various nontechnical or semitechnical senses, in addition to the technical sense in which it is being used here. In one of these semitechnical senses, a powerful theory is one that accounts for a large body of data and does so with maximum simplicity and elegance; and, in this sense of "powerful," the more powerful a theory is, the better it is. But suppose we think of some proposed model of universal grammar (in the sense in which universal grammar is opposed to language-particular grammars) as a theory whose aim it is to distinguish natural languages, actual and potential, from other systems, which (whether they are used for communication or not) might be thought to resemble natural languages in terms of their formal properties. Looked at from this point of view, our model would be too powerful if it generated, in addition to all actual and potential natural languages, systems that we have reason to believe are neither actual nor potential languages. What we are after, therefore, is not the most powerful kind of generative grammar but a generative grammar that is just powerful enough to do what it is required to do.

It has long been suspected that, unless they are restricted in some way, transformational grammars are far too powerful; and this has now been proved to be the case in connection with the universal base hypothesis, to which reference was made earlier in this chapter. In a series of important papers, P. S. Peters and R. W. Ritchie show that any natural language (not to mention systems that are neither actual nor potential natural languages) can be generated by a transformational grammar that contains any one of an infinite number of base components. There is a trivial sense, therefore, in which every natural language can be said to have the same base component. In order to give empirical content to the universal base hypothesis (within the framework of transformational grammar), more specific restrictions must be imposed on the base component or the transformational component than are imposed by the standard theory. Indeed, it is now generally accepted that, whether one wishes to defend some version of the universal base hypothesis or not (and Chomsky, as we have seen, does not), transformational grammar, in any of its Chomskyan or post-Chomskyan forms, is far too powerful for the description of natural languages, unless it is restricted in some way. Much of the most interesting theoretical work that is currently being done, by Chomsky and others, in the field of transformational grammar has as its goal that of imposing on either the base component or the transformational component (or both) conditions that are (as Chomsky puts it in one of his most recent papers) "explicit and as restrictive as possible." The reason is clear: "We want universal grammar to make as strong a statement as possible about the nature of language and thus to be subject to critical tests and to provide explanations for the phenomena attested in descriptive study."

Basic research of this kind is very much in the spirit of Chomsky's earliest work on what he referred to, at that time, as "the logical structure of linguistic theory." It is my contention, throughout this book, that Chomsky's most original contribution to linguistics lies in his having promoted such research and having made clear its significance.

Twenty years after the publication of *Syntactic Structures*, the status of transformational grammar is still a matter of controversy among linguists; and, as we have seen in this chapter, there are now several alternative Chomskyan and post-Chomskyan versions of transformational grammar. It should be added that, although we have not dealt with it here, Zellig Harris's system of transformational grammar, very different from Chomsky's, has also been modified and extended by its author since it was first developed in the mid-1950s. Several other kinds of generative grammar also have been, and are being, proposed: *applicational grammar* (S. K. Shaumjan), *systemic grammar* (M. A. K. Halliday, R. A. Hudson, and others), *stratificational grammar* (S. M. Lamb). It is difficult to compare these and other comprehensive models of linguistic description in terms of their power with the more obviously Chomskyan and post-Chomskyan versions of transformational grammar. Any such comparison presupposes that the grammars in question have been formalized within a common framework, but this is not the case. We have naturally restricted our attention in this chapter to what has just been described as the "more obviously Chomskyan and post-Chomskyan versions of transformational grammar," but any reader who looks farther into this question can readily verify for himself the statement that I made in the Introduction and repeated near the beginning of this chapter to the effect that all current work in theoretical linguistics carries, to a greater or lesser degree, the mark of Chomsky's influence.

The Psychological Implications of Generative Grammar

ix

As I emphasized in Chapter iv, the earlier works of Chomsky were written within the tradition of "autonomous" linguistics. It was only later, in *Aspects of the Theory of Syntax, Cartesian Linguistics*, and *Language and Mind,* that he began to refer to linguistics as a branch of cognitive psychology and to insist upon the importance of generative grammar for the investigation of the structure and predispositions of the human mind. However, as I said in Chapter i, it is for these later views, rather than for his more technical contributions to linguistics as an independent discipline, that Chomsky is now best known. I shall therefore devote this chapter and the next to an exposition of Chomsky's current views on these psychological and philosophical issues, dividing the material, somewhat arbitrarily as it will appear, between the two headings of "psychology" and "philosophy."

Although Chomsky's general position in *Syntactic Structures* is, as far as he reveals it, indistinguishable from that of the "Bloomfieldians" and other empiricists, there is one point on which he has disagreed with Bloomfield and many of his followers from very early on. (I am not now referring to Chomsky's rejection of "discovery" in favor of "evaluation." This issue, which we discussed in a previous chapter, though important in the postwar development of linguistics, is in principle independent of the empiricist position.) Bloomfield, as we have seen, was a behaviorist (at the time that he wrote *Language*), and many of his followers shared his belief that a "mechanistic" account of language in terms of "stimulus and response" was more objective and more scientific than the traditional "mentalistic" description of language as a vehicle for the "expression of thought." In the year that *Syntactic Structures* was published, B. F. Skinner's *Verbal Behavior* also appeared; and it was reviewed in due course by Chomsky. Skinner (now retired from his position as Professor of Psychology at Harvard University) is one of the most eminent and most influential advocates of behaviorist psychology alive at the present time, and his book constitutes the most detailed attempt that has yet been made to account for the acquisition of language within the framework of behavioristic "learning theory." Chomsky's review is now a classic, in which he not only subjects Skinner's book to a penetrating examination but at the same time reveals his own mastery of the relevant psychological literature.

Chomsky has since repeated his arguments against behaviorism on many occasions. Briefly, they amount to the following. One of the most striking facts about language is its "creativity"—the fact that by the age of five or six children are able to produce and understand an indefinitely large number of utterances that they have not previously encountered—and the behaviorist's "learning theory," however successful it might be in accounting for the way in which certain networks of "habits" and "associations" are built up in the "behavior patterns" of animals and human beings, is totally incapable of explaining "creativity"—an aspect of human "behavior" manifest most clearly (though perhaps not exclusively) in language. Chomsky further claims that the terminology of behaviorism ("stimulus," "response," "habit," "conditioning," "reinforcement," etc.), although it can be made precise (and has been made precise in its application to more restricted domains), is so loose as actually applied to language that it could cover anything and is thus completely devoid of empirical content. In the absence of any overt "response," the behaviorist takes refuge in an unobserved and unobservable "disposition to respond"; and having accounted, in principle, for the association of words (as "responses") with objects (as "stimuli") and for the learning of a limited set of sentences in the same way, he either says nothing at all about the formation of new sentences or at this point appeals to some undefined notion of "analogy."

Chomsky's criticisms of behaviorism are undoubtedly valid. It does not follow, of course (and as far as I know Chomsky has never claimed that it does), that no aspects of language, or the use of language, can be reasonably described in terms of a "stimulus and response" model. There can be little doubt, however, that the behaviorist account of the acquisition of language, as formulated at present, fails to come to grips with, let alone solve, the problem posed by what Chomsky calls "creativity."

Neither the earlier nor the later versions of transformational grammar are presented by Chomsky as psychological models of the way people construct and understand utterances. The grammar of a language, as conceived by Chomsky, is an idealized description of the linguistic *competence* of native speakers of that language. (See page 38.) Any psychological model of the way this competence is put to use in actual *performance* will have to take into account a number of additional factors, which the linguist deliberately ignores in his definition of the notion of *grammaticality*. These psychologically relevant factors include the limitations of human memory and attention, the time it takes for neural "signals" to pass from the brain to the muscles that are involved in speech, the interference of one physiological or psychological process with another, and so on. Many of the sentences that the linguist regards as grammatical (well formed in terms of the rules set up to describe the competence of the "ideal" native speaker) would never in fact occur "naturally"; and, if constructed deliberately for the purpose of some linguistic experiment, will be difficult, and perhaps impossible, for actual native speakers to understand, because they cannot be "processed" without "overloading" the various psychological mechanisms involved in the reception and comprehension of speech. This is one way in which the utterances actually produced by speakers of a language might differ significantly, for psychologically explicable reasons, from the sentences described as "grammatical" by the linguist. Another difference, and one that Chomsky has more frequently stressed, is that the utterances produced will contain a variety of mistakes and distortions (mispronunciations, unfinished sentences, hesitations, changes of construction in the middle of a sentence, etc.) due to the malfunctioning of the psychological mechanisms involved or to their inherent limitations. These deviations from the grammatical norm are a valuable part of the psychologist's data and, when properly analyzed, may give him some insight into the structure and operation of the mechanisms underlying the use of language.

Although linguistics and psychology take different points of view with respect to the investigation of language, Chomsky has always maintained that there are important connections between the two disciplines. In fact, the change that one can discern between his earlier and later views of the relationship between psychology and linguistics (to which I have already referred) is largely a matter of emphasis. If Chomsky now describes linguistics as a branch of psychology rather than as an independent discipline, he is not suggesting that the linguist should turn from the investigation of language to the investigation of the use of language, from linguistic competence to linguistic performance. What he is saying is that the most important reason for being interested in the scientific study of language, and especially in generative grammar, is that it has a contribution to make to our understanding of mental processes. Linguistics is incorporated in psychology, therefore, not by virtue of any substantial change in subject matter or method but for the ultimate significance of its results.

Even Chomsky's appeal to "intuition," which is more prominent in his later work (and which has frequently been misunderstood), can be interpreted in this light. According to Chomsky, two grammars may be *observationally* adequate (and weakly equivalent) in that they both generate the same set of sentences. But one will be *descriptively* more adequate than the other if it is in accord with the "intuitions" of native speakers, with respect to such questions as "structural ambiguity" and the equivalence or nonequivalence of certain types of sentences. This is the terminology used in *Aspects of the Theory of Syntax* and in other recent works. The terminological distinction is revealing. It shows that for Chomsky the "intuitions" of the speaker (that is to say, his mental representation of the grammar of the language), rather than the sentences themselves, are the true object of description. As we saw in Chapter iv, Chomsky had previously laid more stress on "sim-

plicity" as a criterion for the evaluation of weakly
equivalent grammars; and, when he did talk of the
speaker's judgments with respect to such questions as
"structural ambiguities," it was never suggested that
these judgments, or "intuitions," were of primary concern; they testified to the informant's apprehension of
the structure of his language, but they did not themselves constitute the subject matter of linguistics. It
is sometimes thought that Chomsky's appeal to the
"intuitions" of the native speaker (including the "intuitions" of the linguist as a speaker of his own native
language) implies some relaxation of the standards of
rigor and objectivity characteristic of "Bloomfieldian"
linguistics and other modern approaches. This is not
so. Chomsky does not claim that the speaker's "intuitions" are immediately accessible; nor does he say that
they are all equally reliable. It is arguable that some
of the work inspired by Chomsky's formulation of the
goals of linguistics rests on a too ready acceptance
of a particular linguist's "intuitions." In principle, however, whether a given sentence is acceptable, whether
it is equivalent to some other sentence or not, and
what its implications are—all these and similar questions that fall within the scope of the native speaker's
"intuition," as Chomsky uses this term—are subject
to empirical verification.

As early as 1958 Chomsky collaborated with the psychologist George Miller in writing a paper entitled
"Finite State Languages," and in 1963 they contributed
two chapters to the *Handbook of Mathematical Psychology* (there is also a further chapter written by Chomsky
alone). One of these chapters by Miller and Chomsky,
"Finitary Models of Language Users," draws in some
detail the implications of generative grammar for the
investigation of the psychological mechanisms underlying linguistic performance.

It follows immediately from Chomsky's proof that

finite-state grammars are incapable of generating some of the sentences to be found in English and other languages, that no performance model based on the same principle of "left-to-right" derivation is worthy of serious consideration. We can therefore exclude all those theories of the production and reception of speech that assume that the probability of occurrence of a given word in a particular position in an utterance is determined solely by the words that have been selected for the preceding positions. It may not seem very plausible that anyone should seek to account for the production of an utterance such as *We have just been running* by saying that the speaker first selects *we* from the set of words permissible at the beginning of English sentences and then, having made this choice, selects *have*, as one of the words that has a certain probability of occurrence after *we*; then, having chosen *we* and *have*, selects *just*, by virtue of its probability of occurrence after *we have*; and so on. Plausible or not (and common-sense "plausibility" is after all not always reliable), this conception of the production of the speech has inspired a considerable amount of psychological research (including, it might be added, some of George Miller's earlier work). Chomsky has proved that this approach is misguided, despite the sophistication of the statistical theory it draws upon.

The second of Chomsky's "models for the description of language" was phrase structure grammar; and, as we saw in Chapter vi, various kinds of phrase structure grammars can be constructed according to the restrictions imposed upon the format or mode of operation of the rules. It is an interesting fact, proved by Chomsky, that context-free phrase structure grammars are equivalent in generative capacity to what are called *push-down storage* devices in *automata theory*. We cannot go into this highly technical question in any detail, but it may be mentioned briefly, in order to give the reader

some idea of the kinds of hypotheses about performance models that can be suggested by a study of the
formal properties of language and the generative
capacity of particular types of grammar.

The human memory, as I said, has presumably only
a finite (though perhaps very large) amount of storage
at its disposal, and it may operate, to some extent at
least, on the "push-down" principle of "last in, first
out," so that, other things being equal, we recall most
easily and most quickly what we have "stored" in
memory most recently. It is reasonable to suppose that
the *long-term*, or permanent, memory contains a good
deal of information, including the rules of the grammar, to which access is made during the "processing"
of utterances. But we are concerned here with what
psychologists call the *short-term memory*, which we
use, for example, when we commit to memory (without
learning or repetition) a list of unconnected items
(e.g., nonsense syllables or digits). There are very
severe limits upon the capacity of short-term memory,
the number of items that we can "store" there being of
the order of seven ("seven plus or minus two," as
Miller put it in the title of a famous paper). So much
is background information relevant to the hypothesis
we are about to discuss.

This is the so-called depth hypothesis, developed in
the early 1960s by Victor Yngve, who was at that time
working on the problems of syntactic analysis by
computer. Let us begin by giving a purely abstract
example of a phrase structure grammar, which includes a number of recursive rules.

(1) A → B + C

(2) B → (B) + D

(3) B → E + (B)

(4) B → F + (B) + G

(5) C → {c, . . .}

(6) D → {d, . . .}

(7) E → {e, . . .}

(8) F → {f, . . .}

(9) G → {g, . . .}

(I have followed a common convention in using capitals for auxiliary elements and lower-case letters for terminal elements.) It will be observed that Rules 2, 3, and 4 are recursive, but in different ways. Rule 2 is *left recursive*; Rule 3 is *right recursive*; and Rule 4 is *self-embedding*. Figures 10, 11, and 12 illustrate what is meant by these terms.

FIGURE 10

FIGURE 11

FIGURE 12

Now, Yngve's hypothesis is that left-recursive structures add to the "depth," or psychological complexity of a sentence, because recursion to the left, unlike recursion to the right, increases the amount of "space" taken up in the short-term memory during the processing of the sentence. When the "depth" of a sentence goes beyond the critical limit (this limit being determined by the capacity of the short-term memory), its continuation becomes unmanageable. And one of the reasons why there are transformations in language, Yngve suggested, is to enable the speaker to avoid excessive "depth" by using equivalent right-branching constructions, rather than left-branching constructions, at certain points in the production of sentences. This hypothesis predicts, therefore, that a phrase like *John's friend's wife's father's gardener's daughter's cat* should be more difficult to "process" than the equivalent right-branching version, *The cat belonging to the daughter of the gardener of the father of the wife of the friend of John.*

The "depth hypothesis," as formulated by Yngve, is almost certainly incorrect, since it rests on the assumption that sentences are "processed" by human beings in the way that they were generated by his computer program. Moreover, it is not clear that left-branching structures are as difficult for human beings to "process" as they should be according to the hypothesis. English has a variety both of left-recursive and right-recursive constructions; and there may well be a general tendency, as Yngve claimed, to avoid excessive "depth" by taking advantage of this fact. But there are other languages, including Turkish and Japanese, where the recursive constructions are predominantly left-branching.

Furthermore, as Chomsky points out in his discussion of Yngve's hypothesis, it is *self-embedding* constructions (as exemplified in Figure 12) that seem to cause the greatest difficulty; and this cannot be explained in terms of the notion of "depth." As a simple example of self-embedding, consider a sentence like *The book the man left is on the table.* Here we have one sentence *The man left the book* (strictly speaking, the string underlying this sentence) embedded in the middle of *The book is on the table* (and subjected to a variety of other operations, including the deletion of *the book* in the embedded relative clause). The resultant complex sentence is perfectly acceptable. But let us now embed yet another sentence in the middle of the previously embedded clause: *The book the man the gardener saw left is on the table*. It is a moot point whether this sentence is acceptable or not. And if we embed a further sentence within *the gardener saw (the man)*, to yield, let us say, *The book the man the gardener I employed yesterday saw left is on the table*, we will surely say that the "output" is unacceptable. Such sentences, despite the formal simplicity of the process of self-embedding, are undeniably difficult to "process" in both the production and the reception of speech. The explanation, as Chomsky says, cannot be simply that there are severe limitations on the capacity of the short-term memory (although this is no doubt one of the factors involved), because *self*-embedding constructions are significantly more difficult to "process" than other constructions derived by the embedding of one element in the middle, rather than at the left or right of a string. In other words, all structures generated by means of a rule of the form $X \rightarrow V + (Y) + W$ (where V and W are strings of one or more elements) involve the temporary "storage" of W while Y is being "processed." Self-embedding occurs when a rule has the more specific property that X and Y take the same "value" (as in Rule 4, page 111). The identity of X and Y appears to introduce additional complexity from the point of view of production and comprehension. Chomsky and Miller suggest, as a hypothesis capable in principle of explaining this fact, that the underlying psychological mechanism is of such a kind that it cannot, or can only with difficulty, execute a particular operation if it is already in the midst of executing the same operation.

More recent research would tend to suggest that neither Yngve's "depth" hypothesis nor Chomsky's hypothesis about self-embedding is of itself sufficient to explain the phenomena. The important point, for present purposes, is that the investigation of the formal properties of language, in terms of notions that derive from generative grammar, has implications for the study of the psychological "mechanisms" and processes underlying linguistic performance. Psychologists were not slow to perceive these implications. George Miller's collaboration with Chomsky in the late 1950s has already been mentioned, and Miller's authority and reputation as a psychologist were such that his colleagues could not but take seriously what was, for most of them, a radically novel way of looking at language.

By the early 1960s, the whole new subdiscipline of *psycholinguistics* had come into being. It has been gathering strength ever since. The term "psycholinguistics" antedates by about a decade the birth of what I have just referred to as a whole new subdiscipline. Psychologists had long been interested in language; and "Bloomfieldian" linguistics, as we have seen, had been strongly influenced by behaviorist psychology. When the term "psycholinguistics" was first used, it referred to a rather loose interdisciplinary synthesis of current psychology and linguistics—a synthesis in which, for a short while, "information theory" seemed capable of having a strong catalyzing effect. (See Chapter v.) Psycholinguistics is something very different nowadays. Whether it is more properly regarded as a subdiscipline of psychology or of linguistics, or alternatively as a hybrid that is part equally of both, is a question of secondary importance. What distinguishes the new psycholinguistics from the old is the very intimacy of the association between psychology and linguistics in what can rightly be described as the new subdiscipline psycholinguistics. It was the revolutionary impact of Chomsky's ideas, more than anything else, that created this new subdiscipline. Not surprisingly, some of the earliest of the distinctively new psycholinguistic work was designed to establish the psychological validity of transformational rules.

As we saw in the previous chapter, the way in which Chomsky accounted for the relationship between corresponding active and passive sentences, corresponding affirmative and negative sentences, corresponding declarative and interrogative sentences, and so on, was by means of a set of optional transformational rules (one of which, the passive transformation, we have studied in some detail). Under this analysis, kernel sentences (simple, affirmative, active, declarative sentences, such as *John was reading a book*) were simpler in terms of the number of rules applied than non-kernel sentences. It was tempting to postulate that kernel sentences were not only linguistically simpler (i.e., in terms of a particular model of competence) but also psychologically simpler, and, assuming a close correspondence between competence and performance, to set up experiments designed to test the psychological validity of transformational processes.

The results of some of the earlier experiments were very encouraging. It was shown, for example, that active sentences could be remembered more easily than passive sentences, and affirmative sentences more easily than negative sentences. Even more strikingly, in an experiment based on the time taken to respond to different types of sentences, it was demonstrated not only that the "latencies," or reaction times, were longer for passive sentences and negative sentences but that the difference between the latency for corresponding affirmative active sentences and negative passive sentences was equal to the sum of the differences for affirmative active and affirmative passive sentences, on the one hand, and for affirmative active and negative active sentences, on the other. This could be interpreted as a confirmation of the hypothesis that the "processing" of sentences included a set of transformational operations, each of which took a certain fixed amount of time to carry out.

These experiments were, in fact, vitiated by a failure

to take into account a number of relevant factors. However we describe the difference between active and passive sentences in English, it is quite clear that the greater "naturalness" of one rather than the other depends upon the kinds of noun phrases or nouns that occur as the underlying subject and object, whether they are definite or indefinite, whether they refer to human beings or things, etc. For instance, *John was reading a book* is more "natural" than *A book was being read by John*, but the passive sentence *John was hit by a car* is more "natural" than the corresponding active sentence *A car hit John*. Unless the corresponding active and passive sentences in an experiment of the kind referred to above are equally "natural," one cannot be sure what is the source of the additional psychological complexity that is being measured by the differences in the latencies. A further potentially relevant factor is the difference in the length of corresponding active and passive sentences. Any experiment that is designed to test the psychological validity of a particular grammatical model must evidently control all the relevant, or potentially relevant, performance variables, as far as these can be determined. By the mid-1960s, psychologists whose research was directly inspired by generative grammar had become more aware of this problem.

Meanwhile, the earliest version of Chomskyan transformational grammar had given way to the *Aspects* system, which had obvious advantages for psycholinguistics. It was more comprehensive and more clearly articulated; and, most important of all, it gave explicit recognition to the process of semantic interpretation. Even if theoretical linguistics could get along well enough by treating languages as purely formal systems, psycholinguistics could not. It had become evident during the earlier period of psycholinguistic research not only that there was no direct correspondence between transformational complexity and psychological complexity (insofar as this could be determined by controlled experiment) but also that it is difficult, if not impossible, to separate syntactic processing from semantic processing. Even if there is a distinction to be drawn between two kinds of psychological process-ing—which is, to say the least, debatable—there is no reason to suppose that the comprehension of an utter-ance involves going through a full-scale syntactic analysis. It is more plausible to hypothesize that the hearer operates with various perceptual "strategies" and surface-structure "cues" as he extracts from the acoustic signal the message that it contains—that is, in terms of the standard theory of *Aspects*, as he determines the deep structure of the sentence that is uttered.

What we may think of as the second period of Chomskyan psycholinguistic research is characterized, then, by a greater interest in semantics and by recog-nition of the importance of taking into account all the information, contextual and acoustic, that the hearer can bring to bear upon the task of interpreting an utterance. The fact that both the production and the comprehension of utterances are temporally ordered processes, subject to modification at various stages before completion, was seen once more as a fact of crucial significance, as it had been ten or fifteen years earlier in the heyday of "information theory." It was no longer possible, however, to suppose that either production or comprehension could be accounted for in terms of a finite-state processor operating "from left to right," and word by word, and making reference to no more than the transitional probabilities of occur-rence. (See Chapter v.) A complete syntactic analysis of the incoming signal might not be necessary. But it was by now clear that the heuristic "strategies" with which the "on-line" processor operates must be able to draw, at times at least, upon a knowledge of syntactic interdependencies that a transformational grammar of the *Aspects* type would handle at the level of deep structure. Such experiments as were carried out during this second period of Chomskyan psycholinguistic research with the aim of demonstrating the psychological reality or unreality of standard-theory deep structures were inconclusive. So too were experiments of various kinds designed to test the psychological validity of the standard-theory formalization of the meaning of words in terms of sets of allegedly universal features.

We are now in the midst of what we may think of, in the present context, as the third period of Chomskyan—and post-Chomskyan—psycholinguistic research. As we saw in the preceding chapter, there are now a considerable number of competing models of generative grammar from which psycholinguistics can choose. But none of them has yet been developed in sufficient detail for it to be made the basis of precisely formulated general psycholinguistic hypotheses. Indeed, it is probable that most psycholinguists have by now realized that the definitive generative model of linguistic competence is something that, if it is ever to be constructed, will not be constructed in the near future. They can be much more eclectic, therefore, in their attitude to what is currently exciting the interest and imagination of theoretical linguists, and that is all to the good! Chomsky, for one, has always stressed the complexity of the relationship between grammatical competence and language performance.

One of the most productive areas of Chomskyan and post-Chomskyan psycholinguistic research in the last fifteen years or so has been the study of children's language acquisition. It would be impossible even to summarize here either the results of this research or the various theoretical controversies by which it has been influenced. But one general point can, and must, be made, in view of the philosophical issue of nativism, which we shall be discussing in the next chapter. All the clearly interpretable evidence that has been collected and studied by workers in the field of children's language acquisition is consistent with Chomsky's nativism. But it cannot be said to give particularly strong positive support to it. All children, it would appear, pass through roughly comparable stages in the process of learning (or, as many specialists prefer to say, acquiring) their native language: the babbling stage, the one-word ("holophrastic") stage, the two-word stage, and so on. This is in itself hardly surprising, and it is consistent with almost every conceivable hypothesis about the determinants of language acquisition. What is more interesting is the fact that at each of the discernibly distinct stages in the process of language acquisition all children (regardless of the cultural and socio-economic environment in which they are being brought up and independently of the language that they hear about them) produce utterances of similar structure at the same stage of development. It may be tempting to see this fact as evidence for the hypothesis that children are born with a language-acquisition device (LAD), which includes the genetically transmitted knowledge of what Chomsky refers to as *formal* and *substantive universals*. (See Chapter x.) But there are alternative explanations.

One of these is that, although there is no language-acquisition device as such (in other words, no device that is restricted to the acquisition of language and is species-specific, in the biologist's sense of being both common to all members of the species and unique to that species), the child is born with a set of species-specific problem-solving "strategies," and with biologically determined limitations on the maturation of these "strategies" and on the development of the psychological "equipment" (memory, etc.) involved in language processing. This is still a "nativist" hypothesis; but, as we shall see, it is not Chomsky's.

Perhaps the fairest evaluation of the situation is to say that such results as have been obtained so far in the investigation of children's language acquisition speak neither for nor against the existence of a genetically transmitted language-acquisition device of the kind Chomsky postulates in *Aspects* and elsewhere.

One final point should be made in this connection. As we saw in Chapter viii, Chomsky has never committed himself to the universal base hypothesis. Passages can be quoted from his writings that suggest that, for a time at least, he flirted with it; but he has always rested his case for nativism on a rather different, and less traditional, conception of universal grammar. We shall be looking at this in the next chapter. What needs to be said here is that, insofar as Chomsky's case for nativism rests, empirically, on the speed with which the child accomplishes the task of language acquisition on the basis of partly degenerate data, it is now generally taken to be weaker than it seemed to be, to many psycholinguists, when he first put forward his views on this question in the mid-1960s. The process of language acquisition lasts several years, and the utterances that the child hears around him may not contain as many instances of ungrammatical strings of words as Chomsky has been taken to be suggesting. Rightly or wrongly, many psycholinguists feel that this makes language acquisition essentially less mysterious and more amenable to explanation, at least in principle, in terms of the maturation of more general cognitive abilities.

Chomsky's influence on the investigation of the acquisition of language is not as strong now, or as direct, as it was in the second period of psycholinguistic research. Far less attention is now being paid to the acquisition of purely grammatical competence, and correspondingly more attention to the acquisition of all that is systematic and of communicative value in what Chomsky describes, in *Aspects*, as performance. However, if Chomsky's influence on the course of psycholinguistic research is, in this respect and in general, less evident than it once was, this is only because psycholinguists have, for the most part, conceded the main point that Chomsky was making when he first attacked the behaviorists' approach to the psychology of language for its pseudoscientific bias and its failure to come to grips with any of the real problems.

The Philosophy of Language and Mind

We now turn from the psychological to the more philosophical implications of generative grammar. It should be remembered, however, that this distinction I am drawing is, as I said at the beginning of the previous chapter, somewhat arbitrary. For it is part of Chomsky's case that linguistics, psychology, and philosophy are no longer to be regarded as separate and autonomous disciplines.

Chomsky believes that linguistics can make an important contribution to the study of the human mind and that, even now, it provides evidence in favor of one position rather than the other in the long-standing philosophical dispute between *rationalists* and *empiricists*. The difference between these two doctrines, at its most extreme, is as follows: The rationalist claims that the mind (or "reason"—hence the term "rationalism") is the sole source of human knowledge; the empiricist, that all knowledge derives from experience.

("Empiricism" comes from the Greek word for "experience.") But there are, of course, less extreme formulations of the difference; and in the long history of Western philosophy the debate between representatives of the two camps has taken a variety of forms.

In the seventeenth and eighteenth centuries, and in a good deal of European and American philosophy since then, one of the main points at issue has been the relationship between the mind (if there is such a thing, as many empiricists would deny) and our perception of the external world. Is this simply a matter of the passive registration of sense impressions and their subsequent combination in terms of laws of "association," as the British empiricists Locke, Berkeley, and Hume claimed was the case? Or should we say, rather, with such philosophers as Descartes, that our perception and understanding of the external world rests upon a number of "ideas" (that is, the knowledge of certain propositions and certain principles of interpretation) and that these "ideas" are "innate," and not derived from experience? The empiricist doctrine has been very influential in the development of modern psychology; and, combined with *physicalism* and *determinism*, it has been responsible for the view, held by many psychologists, that human knowledge and human behavior are wholly determined by the environment, there being no radical difference in this respect between human beings and other animals, or indeed between animals and machines. (By "physicalism" is meant, in this context, the philosophical system according to which all statements made about a person's thoughts, emotions, and sensations can be reformulated as statements about his bodily condition and observable behavior, and can thus be brought within the scope of "physical" laws; by "determinism" is meant the doctrine that all physical events and phenomena, including those actions and decisions of human beings that we might describe as resulting from "choice" or "free will," are determined by earlier events and phenomena and are subject to the laws of cause and effect, so that our impression of freedom of choice is totally illusory. Behaviorism, to which reference was made in the discussion of Bloomfield's theory of language in Chapter iii, is therefore a particular version of physicalism and determinism.) Chomsky's view of man is very different: He believes that we are endowed with a number of specific faculties (to which we give the name "mind") that play a crucial role in our acquisition of knowledge and enable us to act as free agents, undetermined (though not necessarily unaffected) by external stimuli in the environment. These are the issues that Chomsky deals with in his philosophical writings, most notably in *Cartesian Linguistics*, *Language and Mind*, and *Problems of Knowledge and Freedom*. Before plunging into these deep and turbulent waters, it will be as well to discuss the linguistic evidence to which Chomsky appeals as a support for his rationalist philosophy.

As we have seen, "Bloomfieldian" linguistics was remarkably, and at times almost ostentatiously, uninterested in general theoretical questions. Most American linguists (and many linguists in other parts of the world too, it must be admitted), if they had been asked, ten or fifteen years ago, what was the main purpose of linguistics, would probably have said that it was "to describe languages"; and they might well have referred to the practical advantages of a training in the subject for anthropologists, missionaries, and others whose business it was to communicate with peoples speaking a language for which grammars had not yet been written. They would have left the matter at that. Very few of them, if any, would have given the kind of answer to this question that Sapir had suggested in his book *Language*, published a generation before: that language is worth studying because it is unique to man and indispensable for thought.

Indeed, they might well have challenged the propriety of using the word "language" in the singular in the way that I have just done, since this tends to imply that all languages have something in common, and the "Bloomfieldians," as we have seen, were rather skeptical on this point. Bloomfield himself had said, in a much quoted passage, that "the only useful generalizations about language are inductive generalizations," and that "features which we think ought to be universal may be absent from the very next language that becomes accessible."

Chomsky's attitude, as expressed in his most recent publications, is radically opposed to Bloomfield's. He holds that it is the central purpose of linguistics to construct a deductive theory of the structure of human language that is at once sufficiently general to apply to all languages (and not only all known languages but also all possible languages—we will come back to this) and not so general that it would also be applicable to other systems of communication or anything else that we should not wish to call languages. In other words, linguistics should determine the universal and essential properties of human language. In fact, Chomsky's position on this point is similar, as he acknowledges, to that of the Russian linguist Roman Jakobson, who has resided in the United States for a number of years and has long been one of the most outspoken critics of the "Bloomfieldian" tradition.

Like Jakobson, Chomsky believes that there are certain phonological, syntactic, and semantic units that are *universal*, not in the sense that they are necessarily present in all languages but in the somewhat different, and perhaps less usual, sense of the term "universal," that they can be defined independently of their occurrence in any particular language and can be identified, when they do occur in particular languages, on the basis of their definition within the general theory. For example, it is held that there is a fixed set of up to twenty *distinctive features* of phonology (e.g., the feature of *voicing* that distinguishes *p* from *b* or *t* from *d* in the pronunciation of the English words *pin* and *bin* or *ten* and *den*, or the feature of *nasality* that distinguishes *b* from *m* or *d* from *n* in *bad* and *mad* or *pad* and *pan*). Not all of these will be found in the phonemes of all languages; but from their various possible combinations every language will, as it were, make its own selection. Similarly at the level of syntax and semantics. Such syntactic categories as Noun or Verb or Past Tense, and such components of the meaning of words as "male" or "physical object," belong to fixed sets of elements, in terms of which it is possible to describe the syntactic and semantic structure of all languages, although no particular language will necessarily manifest all the elements recognized as "universal" in the general theory. These phonological, syntactic, and semantic elements are what Chomsky calls the *substantive universals* of linguistic theory.

Far more characteristic of Chomsky's thought, and more original, is his emphasis on what he refers to as *formal universals*, that is, the general principles that determine the form of the rules and the manner of their operation in the grammars of particular languages. For example, the transformations that relate various sentences and constructions, Chomsky claims, "are invariably *structure-dependent* in the sense that they apply to a string of words by virtue of the organization of these words into phrases."[1] All the transformations that we discussed in Chapter vii (and notably the passive transformation) satisfy this condition, since, as we saw, their applicability was determined by the analyzability of the "input" string with reference to the associated phrase marker (and this is what Chomsky means by "structure-dependency"). It is an important fact about language, says Chomsky,

[1] *Language and Mind*, p. 51.

that it does not make use of structure-independent operations in order to relate one sentence type, let us say, to another. For example, the relationship between the declarative sentence *John was here yesterday* and the corresponding interrogative *Was John here yesterday?* might seem at first sight to be describable in terms of a simple operation permuting the first and second words (with an accompanying change of intonation, which we will neglect here). This operation would be structure-independent, if it were specified by means of a rule that made no reference to the syntactic function of *John* and *was*. Consideration of a wider class of examples (such as *His elder brother was here yesterday* and *Was his elder brother here yesterday?*, *The blast-off took place on time* and *Did the blast-off take place on time?*) shows us that the rule must be expressed somewhat as follows (to put it informally): "Permute the whole of the subject noun phrase with the first auxiliary verb, introducing the auxiliary verb *do* for the purpose, when there is no other." It thus turns out that those sentences, like *John was here yesterday* and *Was John here yesterday?*, which can be related by means of a rule of the form "Permute the first two words," also fall within the scope of the more general structure-dependent rule; it just happens that the subject noun phrase is a single word and occupies the first position of the declarative sentence and the second word is an auxiliary verb. According to Chomsky, it will always prove to be the case that what appear to be valid structure-independent operations are special instances of more general structure-dependent operations.

Chomsky and his associates have tentatively proposed a number of more specific universal constraints upon the operation of grammatical rules. Limitations of space prevent me from mentioning more than one of these. I shall take what Chomsky calls the "A-over-A" principle (which is one of the three constraints he dis-

cusses in *Language and Mind*). This means that, if a
transformational rule makes reference to a phrase of
type A and the string of elements to which the rule
applies contains two such phrases, one being included
within the other, the rule will operate only upon the
larger phrase. (In the associated phrase marker the
larger phrase of type A dominates the phrase of type
A that it includes.) Obvious examples of strings of
elements that come within the scope of this principle
are noun phrases that contain noun phrases. For
instance, *the book on the desk* is a noun phrase, and
the desk, which is included within it, is also a noun
phrase. According to the "A-over-A" principle, any
rule that moves, deletes, or otherwise operates upon
noun phrases could apply to the whole phrase *the
book on the desk*, but not to *the desk*. There are a number of facts in the grammar of English and other
languages that appear to be satisfactorily explained in
terms of this general principle. On the other hand, as
Chomsky points out, there are certain rules that violate
the principle, although they appear to be otherwise well
motivated; and in the present state of research it is not
clear whether the "A-over-A" principle should just be
abandoned or whether it is possible to modify it in
such a way that it will cover the exceptions also. And
this seems to hold for all the more specific constraints
that have been proposed so far: They are only partially
satisfactory, since they explain only some of the
relevant data. Although the "A-over-A" principle, as it
is at present formulated, is, by Chomsky's own ad-
mission, probably not valid, it will serve as an illus-
tration of the kind of constraints upon the application
of grammatical rules that Chomsky has in mind when
he talks of the formal universals of linguistic theory.

It may be worth pointing out that, as far as substantive universals are concerned, Chomsky's view is
not necessarily in conflict with Bloomfield's, since
Chomsky accepts that any one of his allegedly uni-

versal features might be absent not only "from the very next language that becomes accessible" but also from very many quite familiar languages. It is for this reason I referred earlier to the difference between Chomsky's view of "universals" and the "Bloomfieldian" view as one of "attitude." Bloomfield and his "structuralist" disciples, for reasons that were explained in Chapter iii, followed Boas in stressing the diversity of human languages; Chomsky emphasizes their similarities. Clearly, one must give due recognition to the differences of grammatical structure that are found throughout the languages of the world. But there can be little doubt that the "Bloomfieldians," as well as many other schools of linguists, in their anxiety to avoid the bias of traditional grammar, have tended to exaggerate these differences and have given undue emphasis to the principle that every language is a law unto itself. The grammatical similarities that exist between widely separated and historically unrelated languages are at least as striking as their differences. Moreover, recent work in the syntactic analysis of a number of languages lends support to the view that the similarities are deeper and the differences more superficial.

As we saw in Chapter ix, Chomsky himself has been more cautious than some of his followers in accepting that languages are more similar in their deep structure than they are in their surface structure. He attaches far more importance to the fact (and let us grant, provisionally, that it is a fact) that different languages make use of the same formal operations in the construction of grammatical sentences. And it is upon this kind of similarity between languages, as we shall see presently, that he rests his case for a rationalist philosophy of language.

It will be recalled that finite-state grammars and phrase structure grammars were criticized by Chomsky as being insufficiently powerful for the description of natural languages. One of the most obvious deficiencies of current versions of transformational grammar, as Chomsky has pointed out, is that they are *too* powerful. (See Chapter viii and Appendix 1.) There is an extremely important principle involved here, and it is essential to an understanding of Chomsky's notion of "universal grammar." When we discussed "the goals of linguistic theory" in Chapter iv, we saw that the linguist, in writing a generative grammar of a particular language, sets himself the task of characterizing "all and only" the sentences of that language. (This is of course an ideal, at present unrealized for any natural language; but this does not affect the principle.) The same point holds on the more general plane. Linguistic theory, as we have seen, should be both general enough to cover all particular languages and yet not so general that it will apply to other systems of communication (and thereby define them implicitly as "languages"). Transformational grammar, in its present form, allows for the possibility of a variety of operations and various ways of building up sequences of operations that, as far as we know, are not required for the description of any human language. This means that it is more general than it need be as a theory of the structure of human language. The problem is to decide whether there are any formal limitations that we can incorporate in the theory of transformational grammar such that the grammars of particular languages written within these deliberately imposed limitations will not only be in principle capable of accounting for all the sentences that are actually found in those languages but will exclude as *theoretically* impossible the maximum number of nonsentences. As we have seen, Chomsky believes that there are certain very specific conditions that govern the operation of grammatical rules in all languages; and it is by means of these conditions, provided that they can be determined and formalized, that he proposes to restrict the power of transformational grammar.

We now come to the philosophical consequences of Chomsky's notion of universal grammar. If all human languages are strikingly similar in structure, it is natural to ask why this should be so. It is equally natural, or so it might appear to an empiricist philosopher, to answer this question by appealing to such obviously relevant facts as the following: All human languages make reference to the properties and objects of the physical world, which, presumably, is perceived in essentially the same way by all physiologically and psychologically normal human beings; all languages, in whatever culture they might operate, are called upon to fulfill a similar range of functions (making statements, asking questions, issuing commands, etc.); all languages make use of the same physiological and psychological "apparatus," and the very way in which this operates may be held responsible for some of the formal properties of language. Now all these facts are, as I have said, relevant; and they may well have exerted an influence upon the structure of language. But many of the universal features of language, both substantive and formal, are not readily explained in this way. The only conceivable explanation, says Chomsky, in terms of our present knowledge at least, is that human beings are genetically endowed with a highly specific "language faculty" and that it is this "faculty" that determines such universal features as structure-dependency or the "A-over-A" principle (to take the two examples mentioned earlier in this chapter). It is at this point that Chomsky makes contact with the rationalist tradition in philosophy.

Chomsky's conclusion is reinforced, he claims, by a consideration of the process by which children learn their native language. All the evidence available suggests that children are not born with a predisposition to learn any one language rather than any other. We may therefore assume that all children, regardless of race and parentage, are born with the same ability for learning languages; and, in normal circumstances, children will grow up as what we call "native speakers" of the language that they hear spoken in the community in which they are born and spend their early years. But how does the child manage to develop the creative command of his native language that enables him to produce and understand sentences he has never heard before? As we have seen, Chomsky maintains that it is only by assuming that the child is born with a knowledge of the highly restrictive principles of universal grammar, and the predisposition to make use of them in analyzing the utterances he hears about him, that we can make any sense of the process of language learning. Empiricist theories of language learning cannot bridge the gap between the relatively small number of utterances (many of them full of errors, distortions, and hesitations) that the child hears about him and his ability to construct for himself on the basis of these scanty and imperfect data, in a relatively short time, the grammatical rules of the language. It is the child's inborn knowledge of the universal principles governing the structure of human language that supplies the deficiency in the empiricist account of language acquisition. These principles are part of what we call the "mind," being represented in some way, no doubt, in the structure or mode of operation of the brain, and may be compared with the "innate ideas" of Descartes and the rationalist tradition going back to Plato.

It was pointed out toward the end of the preceding chapter that the balance of opinion seems to have shifted in the last few years toward the view that the so-called primary data (the utterances to which the child is exposed) are not as degenerate as Chomsky has frequently been understood to have suggested. It is only fair to add here that Chomsky claims that he has been misrepresented and misunderstood on this matter: "Just how degenerate is this experience? I know of no reliable evidence, but the problem appears to have been misunderstood, and some incorrect statements have been made about what has been asserted. As for the problem, suppose that a scientist were presented with data, 2% of which are wrong (but he doesn't know which 2%). Then he faces some serious difficulties, which would be incomparably more serious if the data were simply uncontrolled experience, rather than the result of controlled experiment, devised for its relevance to theoretical hypotheses."[2] Chomsky goes on to say that he has never asserted that "the great majority of the sentences that the child hears are ungrammatical," and that he has never given any "quantitative estimates."

As the quotation in the previous paragraph makes clear, Chomsky considers that, in the circumstances in which children acquire their native language, the presence of even a relatively small number of ungrammatical utterances in the "primary" data constitutes a serious problem for any purely empiricist theory of language acquisition. In view of the difference of opinion that exists between Chomsky and his empiricist critics on this particular question, it is worth reemphasizing the fact that many of the psychologists working in the field of language acquisition who disagree with Chomsky with respect to the plausibility of the hypothesis that children have an inborn knowledge of the principles of universal grammar would nonetheless agree with him when he says that purely empiricist theories of language acquisition are incapable of explaining the facts.

Chomsky's theory of transformational grammar was originally formulated, as I have stressed throughout this book, within the framework of "autonomous"

[2] "Conditions on Rules of Grammar," footnote 6.

linguistics. Such few references as there are in his earlier writings to philosophical issues would suggest that he, like most other linguists and psychologists, saw no reason to dispute the empiricist theory of knowledge and perception. This fact should be borne in mind in any assessment of his current philosophical views. Having been trained himself in the predominantly empiricist tradition of modern science, he is well aware that his notion of the genetic transmission of the principles of universal grammar will strike many philosophers and scientists as absurdly fanciful. As he pointed out in his radio discussion with Stuart Hampshire: "The empiricist view is so deep-seated in our way of looking at the human mind that it almost has the character of a superstition."[3] After all, we do not accuse the biologist of unscientific mysticism when he postulates the genetic transmission and subsequent maturation of the quite complex "instinctual" behavior patterns characteristic of various species. Why should we be so ready to believe that human behavior, which is demonstrably more complex and more flexible, *must* be accounted for without the postulation of certain highly specialized abilities and dispositions (to which we give the name "mind") with which we are genetically endowed and which manifests themselves, in the appropriate circumstances, at a certain stage of our development?

It is of course the traditional associations of the word "mind" that are responsible for much of the hostile reaction to Chomsky's rationalism (or "mentalism"). Many philosophers, and most notably, perhaps, Descartes, have drawn a very sharp distinction between "body" and "mind"; and they have claimed that the physiological functions and operations of the "body," unlike the workings of the "mind," are subject to the same "mechanical," or "physical," laws as the rest of

[3] Printed in *The Listener*, May 30, 1968.

the "material" world. Chomsky's position is, however, somewhat different. Like Descartes and other "mentalists," he believes that human behavior is, in part at least, undetermined by external stimuli or internal physiological states; he is thus opposed to "mechanism" (or "physicalism," in the usual sense). On the other hand, he differs from Descartes and most philosophers who would normally be called "mentalist" in that he does not subscribe to the ultimate irreducibility of the distinction between "body" and "mind." In the radio interview to which I have referred, he makes the point that "the whole issue of whether there's a physical basis for mental structures is a rather empty issue," because, in the development of modern science, "the concept 'physical' has been extended step by step to cover anything we understand," so that "when we ultimately begin to understand the properties of mind, we shall simply . . . extend the notion 'physical' to cover these properties as well." He does not even deny that it is possible in principle to account for "mental phenomena" in terms of "the physiological processes and physical processes that we now understand." It will be clear from these quotations that, although Chomsky describes himself as a "mentalist," it is mechanistic determinism, and more particularly behaviorism, to which he is opposed, and that, in contrast with such philosophers as Plato or Descartes, he might equally well be described as a "physicalist."

Conclusion

xi

In the previous chapters of this book I have tried to give a clear and sympathetic account of Chomsky's views on language, and I have deliberately refrained from making any kind of critical comment that might hold up or complicate the exposition. I must not leave the reader with the impression, however, that Chomsky's position is impregnable and his critics simply misguided or malevolent. In this final chapter, therefore, I shall redress the balance somewhat by giving a more personal assessment of the significance of Chomsky's work. Although my own views are very similar to Chomsky's on most issues, there are some points on which I think he has overstated his case.

I have already said that it is Chomsky's research on the formalization of syntactic theory that constitutes his most original and probably his most enduring contribution to the scientific investigation of language, and there can be little doubt about this. He has greatly extended the scope of what is called "mathematical linguistics" and opened up a whole field of research, which is of interest not only to linguists but also to logicians and mathematicians. Even if it were decided eventually that none of Chomsky's work on generative grammar was of any direct relevance to the description of natural languages, it would still be judged valuable by logicians and mathematicians, who are concerned with the construction and study of formal systems independently of their empirical application. I shall say no more about this point.

It is, of course, the fact that Chomsky's model of transformational grammar was designed for the analysis of natural languages and has been employed with considerable success for that purpose over the past fifteen or twenty years that has attracted the attention of psychologists and philosophers. Chomsky himself has argued, as we have seen, that the findings of transformational grammar have certain very definite implications for psychology and philosophy. He has made a strong, and to my mind convincing, case against behaviorism (in its extreme form at least); and he has argued, again cogently, that the gap between human language and systems of animal communication is such that it cannot be abridged by any obvious extension of current psychological theories of "learning" based on laboratory experiments with animals. This follows from the principle of "creativity" manifest in the use of language and does not depend, it should be observed, upon the validity of any particular model of generative grammar, or indeed even upon the possibility of constructing one.

At this point, something should be said about the attempts that have been made recently to teach language to chimpanzees and the implications that the results of these experiments have for the Chomskyan version of "nativism." Earlier attempts had been made to teach chimpanzees spoken language, and they had failed. It now appears that the reason for their failure is that chimpanzees simply do not have the same kind of vocal apparatus that human beings have. More recent experiments, therefore, have operated with communication systems that make use of the manual-visual, rather than the vocal-auditory, channel; and they have been remarkably successful. The experiments have been so successful, in fact, that they are now commonly believed to have disproved Chomsky's assertion that "acquisition of even the barest rudiments of language is quite beyond the capacities of an otherwise intelligent ape."[1] Well, have they?

One of the chimpanzees, Washoe, was learning the American Sign Language (ASL), widely used by deaf people in the United States. This is a "logographic," rather than an alphabetic, system, in the sense that it is not based on the principle of finger spelling but has signs each of which can be related directly, and one by one, to individual words (or their meanings). Not only did Washoe succeed in learning more than a hundred signs before she grew too difficult to manage (at the age of six years), but she used the signs appropriately, producing them spontaneously herself and interpreting them correctly when they were produced by others. Even more impressive is the fact that she was able to produce appropriate new sign sequences she had never met before. Admittedly, the sequences were never very long; but they were as long as the spoken utterances of human children at an early stage of language acquisition. It would appear, therefore, that Washoe (unlike, for example, Frisch's honeybees—see Chapter ii) has demonstrated the ability to construct new combinations of discrete units; and this is what we have been calling "creativity."

[1] *Language and Mind*, p. 59.

Sarah, an equally famous chimpanzee, has been learning a rather different communication system— one that, unlike ASL, is not parasitic upon pre-existing human language but was constructed especially for the purpose. Furthermore, unlike Washoe, who acquired her knowledge of ASL by interacting in a more or less natural way with her trainers, Sarah has been taught by means of a systematic program based on the "operant conditioning" principle of behaviorist psychology. Sarah's "language" consists of a set of sentences whose "words" are colored plastic tokens. These are arranged vertically on a magnetic board according to rules established by the inventors of the system. This allows for the construction of both affirmative and negative statements, questions, conditional sentences, and quantified phrases (*some apples, all the apples, no apples*). The syntax of the system is such that it has some degree of structure-dependency, and Sarah appears to have been able to cope with this.

Well, then, have Washoe and Sarah (who are but the first and most famous of what is now quite a large number of chimpanzees who have been involved in such experiments) demonstrated a capacity for language? The answer to this question is unclear. The two chimpanzees have between them shown that certain nonhuman primates are capable of using learning systems that have some degree of rule-governed "creativity" and some degree of structure-dependency. It is open to Chomsky to object, however, that the difference between a fully developed natural language and systems of the kind that Washoe and Sarah have been learning is qualitative, rather than quantitative. Disputes as to what is qualitative and what is quantitative are notoriously difficult to resolve, and many scientists would say that they are rather pointless.

As far as I can see, the results of the experiments

with chimpanzees leave the whole question of the species-specificity of language exactly where it was before; and it is, up to a point, definitional. It has been argued that, if the chimpanzees have not succeeded in acquiring at least the "barest rudiments" of language, children in the earlier stages of language acquisition have not succeeded in acquiring the "barest rudiments" of language either. But the argument as it stands, is fallacious; for children go far beyond the stage at which, so far at least, the chimpanzees stop. According to the Chomskyan hypothesis, this is because children are operating with a species-specific maturational disposition that the chimpanzees lack; and, if this is so, despite the alleged structural similarities between young children's utterances and the utterances of Washoe and other chimpanzees learning ASL, it is legitimate to say that, whereas children are quite obviously acquiring language, the chimpanzees have not demonstrated that they are. Of course, it may yet turn out that chimpanzees, or representatives of some other nonhuman species, will refute the Chomskyan hypothesis by acquiring a communication system with the same kind and the same degree of structure-dependency and rule-governed creativity that human languages have. So far they have not done so.

It is important to realize in this connection that to describe as quantitative what Chomsky might hold to be qualitative is not of itself to solve the problem of accounting for the differences between human languages and other communication systems. It should also be pointed out that there has been a good deal of rather superficial discussion, in popular treatments of the difference between language and nonlanguage, of what have come to be called the *design features*, or general properties, of language. Three of these have been mentioned in this book: *duality*, *creativity*, and *structure-dependency*. Others that might have been mentioned are *arbitrariness* and *discreteness*. All of these, apart from structure-dependency, to which, as we have seen, Chomsky attaches particular importance, appear on a well-known list of sixteen properties drawn up by C. F. Hockett about fifteen years ago. There are two general points that must be made about this list. The first is that it is very heavily weighted in favor of signaling systems that make use of the vocal-auditory channel. It is arguable, however, that language should not be bound, by definition, to transmission through the vocal-auditory channel; and, as we have seen, any claim to the effect that Washoe and Sarah have been acquiring language depends on our acceptance of the fact that transmission through the vocal-auditory channel is not a definitional property of language.

This point is of some importance. There is some evidence to suggest that the two hemispheres of the human brain are involved in rather different aspects of language processing and that, whereas the left hemisphere (in most people) carries out the more characteristically linguistic processes, the right hemisphere deals with the less characteristically linguistic processes, including some of the processing of the vocal signal as such. It is at least conceivable that man's biological predisposition to acquire speech is to be distinguished from his biological predisposition to acquire language (on the assumption that he has both), and it is important to appreciate that evidence for the one cannot be taken as evidence for the other. The two are often confused.

The second point is even more important. Hockett's list of design features is often taken as a checklist of properties that particular signaling systems either have or do not have. Systems are then graded as being more or less similar to natural languages according to the number of features that they share with natural languages. It turns out, for example, that, according to this way of comparing communication systems, the sets of signals used by such birds as thrushes and crows differ from human languages only with respect to the features of *prevarication* (the ability to lie) and *reflectiveness* (the ability to communicate about the system itself). The comparison stands condemned by the absurdity of the results that it yields, and one does not need to look long to see what is wrong with the method of comparison. Not only does each distinguishable feature count equally in the classification, but many of the features are so loosely defined that their identification with similarly named features in natural languages must be rejected. This is arguably the case for open-endedness ("creativity") and it is most certainly the case for semanticity, arbitrariness, discreteness, and duality. Furthermore, it is the degree to which languages have these properties and the way the design features interact with one another that makes of language systems the flexible instruments for communication that they are. Chomsky may be right or wrong about the species-specificity of language, but one thing is clear: What his theory of generative grammar seeks to formalize—rule-governed, structure-dependent creativity whose complexity is defined by the power of the grammar—is certainly an essential part of language.

So much may be said, then, about the vexatious question of the relationship between human language and animal communication systems. It may be worth repeating that, although Chomsky has given good reason to believe that the model of "stimulus and response" is incapable of accounting for *all* the facts of language behavior, he has not shown that it cannot explain *any* of them. It might well be that some of the words referring to objects in the child's environment and certain utterances that occur frequently in the repetitive situations in which he finds himself in early life are learned by him in a way that is quite reasonably described in behaviorist terms (by saying that the words and utterances are "responses" and the objects and situations are "stimuli"); and it could also be true that this part of language not only can, but must, be learned and related to the external world and the world of social activity in this way. As far as I know, there is no evidence to suggest that this view is wrong or even implausible. What Chomsky has demonstrated is that the behaviorist account of language acquisition, if it is not entirely abandoned, must be supplemented with something more substantial than rather empty appeals to "analogy."

But what of the wider philosophical issues that he has raised in his later work? Here I think that the only verdict that can be returned, on the evidence available, is that Chomsky's case for rationalism is not quite as strong as he suggests. It rests, as we have seen, upon the alleged universality of certain formal principles of sentence construction in natural languages; and he is committed to the view "that if an artificial language were constructed which violated some of these general principles, then it would not be learned at all, or at least not learned with the ease and efficiency with which a normal child will learn human language."[2] But this hypothesis, as Chomsky's critics have pointed out, is not subject to direct empirical verification. For it is obviously impracticable to bring up a child from birth with no knowledge of any natural language, exposing him only to utterances in an artificial language spoken in a full range of "normal" situations. Nor is it at all clear how one would go about designing an acceptable psychological experiment bearing less directly upon the issues involved.

Even if we grant for the sake of argument that the formal principles to which Chomsky appeals are uni-

[2] *The Listener*, May 30, 1968, p. 688.

versal in the sense that they do indeed hold in all languages actually spoken by human beings, are we justified in maintaining that they are peculiarly congenial to the human mind, so that any *conceivable* human language *must* conform to them? Since we cannot prove, as yet, that languages violating these principles could not be learned or used by human beings, we are entitled to withhold our assent to Chomsky's hypothesis that these formal universals are innate. An alternative explanation of their universality might be that all languages have a common origin in the remote past and have preserved the formal principles of their source.[3] Whether all existing languages do in fact derive from one source is not known—and, once again, we are faced with what seems to be an unverifiable hypothesis—but it is a possibility that should be allowed for.

Insofar as linguistics is an empirical science whose purpose it is to construct a theory of the structure of human language, it is of course important that linguists should incorporate within the theory all the substantive and formal universals that can be established in the investigation of particular languages. Chomsky is right,

[3] This point is explicitly discussed by Chomsky in *Language and Mind* (pp. 74–75), where he argues that it "involves a serious misunderstanding of the problem at issue." It is true, as he says, that the hypothesis of common origin "contributes nothing to explaining" how "the grammar of a language must be discovered by the child from the data presented to him." But this is not the problem for which the hypothesis of common origin is being proposed here as an explanation. Chomsky's assumption that certain formal principles of grammar are innate is intended to account for two problems simultaneously: (1) the universality of the principles (on the assumption that they are in fact found to be universal) and (2) the child's success in constructing the grammar of his language on the basis of the utterances he hears around him. It is the second of these questions that Chomsky regards as the more important ("the language is 'reinvented' each time it is learned, and the empirical problem to be faced by the theory of learning is how this invention of grammar can take place").

I believe, when he says that the diversity of structures found throughout the languages of the world is less striking than the "structuralists" have claimed. On the other hand, it should be emphasized that relatively few languages have yet been described in any great detail. Syntactic research of recent years, much of it inspired directly by Chomsky's work, seems to me to lend a fair amount of support to the adherents of "universal grammar." But the results that have been obtained so far must be regarded as very tentative, and this fact should be borne in mind when linguistic evidence is being used in philosophical arguments.

It is in any case arguable that some of the old philosophical and psychological oppositions, such as rationalism vs. empiricism, instinct vs. learning, mind vs. body, heredity vs. environment, and so on, have lost much of their force. Current work in the comparative study of animal and human behavior would suggest that behavior that is normally described as "instinctual" requires very particular environment conditions during the period of "maturation." Whether one says that such behavior is "innate" or "learned by experience" is a matter of emphasis; both "instinct" and "environment" are necessary, and neither is sufficient without the other.

As we saw at the end of the last chapter, Chomsky, although he calls himself a "mentalist," does not wish to be committed to the traditional opposition of "body" and "mind." His position would seem to be consistent with the view that the "knowledge" and "predispositions" for language, though "innate," require rather definite environmental conditions during the period of "maturation." One might go on to suggest, as an alternative to Chomsky's hypothesis, that it is not a "knowledge" of the formal principles of language as such that is innate but a more general "faculty," which, given the right environmental conditions, will

interact with these to produce linguistic competence.[4]
This could still be called a "rationalist" hypothesis in
the sense that it contradicts the more extreme form of
empiricism. But then there are probably very few
extreme empiricists. Most philosophers and psychologists would no doubt accept that some "mental
faculties" are specific to human beings (although they
might prefer not to use the words "mental faculty")
and are both biologically and environmentally determined. Once again, it must be admitted that there is
no evidence to show that this alternative hypothesis
(which many scholars who call themselves "empiricists" might favor) is correct. But I am not claiming
that Chomsky is wrong. What I am saying is that the
evidence, so far at least, is inconclusive.

The fact that we have delivered a verdict of "not
proven" on Chomsky's particularly strong form of the
rationalist thesis does not mean that it is without importance. He has shown that there is nothing inherently
unscientific about the assumption, or hypothesis, that
competence in speaking a language implies that the
speaker has in his "mind" a number of generative rules
(whether they are "innate" or "learned") of a highly
restricted kind and is capable of "storing" and operat-

---

[4] Chomsky says that he is not convinced that this is a true
"alternative"; he accepts that the proper environmental
conditions are necessary for the maturation of innate structures (cf., *Aspects of the Theory of Syntax*, pp. 33–34).
He believes that "no more is at stake than a decision as to
how to apply the term 'knowledge' in a rather obscure
area." He further suggests that I should point out that
"even the most narrow empiricist would not regard a
hypothesis as devoid of empirical content because it is not
directly testable in practice," that it is generally accepted
by modern empiricists "that meaningful hypotheses, in
general, must only meet the condition that some possible
evidence have some bearing on them—that they not be
entirely neutral with respect to all conceivable evidence."
I did not intend to give the impression in my criticism of
Chomsky's hypothesis that I regard it as meaningless or
vacuous, but it may be as well to make this point explicit.

ing upon abstract "mental structures" in the course of producing or analyzing utterances. This in itself is a considerable achievement, given the strong prejudice that existed not long ago among psychologists and linguists, and perhaps also philosophers of science, against any theory that went beyond the observable data. Chomsky was surely right to challenge "the belief that the mind must be simpler in its structure than any known physical organ and that the most primitive of assumptions must be adequate to explain whatever phenomena can be observed."[5]

It would be inappropriate in a book of this nature, and impossible in the space available, to give a detailed criticism of Chomsky's theory of generative grammar from a purely linguistic point of view.[6] I must be content with two general points. The first has to do with the distinction he draws between "competence" and "performance," which was mentioned in Chapters iv and ix. Although a distinction of this kind is undoubtedly both a theoretical and a methodological necessity in linguistics, it is by no means certain that Chomsky himself draws it in the right place. It can be argued that he describes as matters of "performance" (and, therefore, as irrelevant) a number of factors that should be handled in terms of "competence." The second point is that, on questions of detail, any linguist's judgment of what is a more "natural" or more "revealing" way of describing the data will tend to be somewhat arbitrary. Furthermore, it is not always clear when the differences between alternative descriptions of the same data are differences of substance and

[5] *Language and Mind*, p. 22.

[6] For a critical discussion of the more technical points in what is now referred to as the standard theory, the reader is referred to P. H. Matthews's review of *Aspects of the Theory of Syntax*. Many of the criticisms carry over to the extended standard theory.

when they are merely differences of terminology and notation.

Both of the points that I have just made require amplification in the light of recent developments. To take first the question of competence and performance: In a famous passage, Chomsky says, "Linguistic theory is concerned primarily with an ideal speaker-listener in a completely homogeneous speech-community, who knows its language (i.e., the language of the community) perfectly and is unaffected by such grammatically irrelevant conditions as memory limitations, distractions, shifts of attention and interest, and errors (random or characteristic) in applying his knowledge of the language (i.e., the language-system) in actual performance."[7] It has been argued by many, and I agree, that Chomsky's use of the term "performance" to cover everything that does not fall within the scope of a deliberately idealized and theoretically restricted notion of linguistic competence is unfortunate. It would have been preferable, in my view, to restrict the notion of "performance" to the production and interpretation of utterances on particular occasions of the use of language and to introduce other distinctions to account for the idealization (cf., "in a completely homogeneous speech-community") and decontextualization (cf., Chomsky's definition of a language as a set of sentences, rather than as a set of appropriately contextualized utterances).

It does not follow, however, from this essentially terminological point that Chomsky's idealization itself is illegitimate; and I do not believe that it is. Linguists can and should give full recognition to differences of dialect and style and to their social and contextual determinants; and it falls within the province of sociolinguistics, both theoretical and descriptive, to do just

[7] *Aspects of the Theory of Syntax*, p. 3.

this. Dell Hymes, who has argued cogently for the
extension of the notion of "competence," makes the
additional point that "a child from whom any and all
of the grammatical sentences might come with equal
likelihood would be . . . a social monster."[8] This is
true, and Chomsky would not wish to deny it. Nor
would he wish to deny the fact of stylistic and dialectic
variation or its positive communicative and social
function. It so happens, however, that what Chomsky
takes, rightly or wrongly, to be the crucial property
of human language can be studied, in his opinion,
without taking socially and contextually determined
variation into account. As far as I know, there is no
reason to dispute what he has to say on this point.
Generative grammarians (though not, I think, Chomsky) may have rested their case for or against the
postulation of some particular grammatical rule upon
data of questionable validity; and, when challenged,
they may have adopted too readily what has been aptly
called the "my-dialect-your-dialect gambit." If so, it is
their cavalier attitude to what should be standard procedures of empirical verification, not the principle of
idealization as such, that is at fault.

This point has been emphasized because there has
recently been a noticeable shift of interest within linguistics from the more narrowly grammatical to the
social and behavioral aspects of language. It is important to realize that, although the sociolinguistic
viewpoint is, for its own purposes, valid, it does not
invalidate the Chomskyan idealization. Neither viewpoint is more "realistic" than the other; they both
involve some kind of idealization (as all empirical
science does); they are equally legitimate, but different.

The second point mentioned above has to do with
the question of terminological and notational differ-

8 *Foundations in Sociolinguistics*, p. 75.

ences. As we saw in Chapter viii, there are now a considerable number of alternative versions of Chomskyan and post-Chomskyan generative grammar. Chomsky has claimed that some of these are no more than "notational variants" of his own system. It is by no means clear that he is right on this issue. The problem is that, whereas the weak equivalence of two grammars is something that is clearly determinable (provided that they have both been fully formalized), the question of strong equivalence is much more complex. Two grammars are said to be strongly equivalent if they assign to the sentences that they generate the same structural descriptions. (Cf., Appendix 1.) The problem is that scholars may disagree as to what is significant and what is not, in the formal representation of the structure of a sentence. Unless the parties to any dispute that has to do with strong equivalence can come to some agreement about the significance or insignificance of terminological and notational variation, the dispute itself is fruitless; and many of the more technical arguments between Chomsky and those who favor some other form of generative grammar have had something of this character.

The comments that have just been made are intended to show that I will not try to justify the two points I have just made. They have been mentioned simply to indicate that even those linguists who are generally sympathetic to Chomsky's views may differ from him on various issues. Other scholars, of course, have more fundamental objections to his theory of generative grammar.

Earlier in this chapter, I said that we must at least envisage the possibility that Chomsky's theory of generative grammar will be dismissed one day, by the consensus of linguists, as irrelevant to the description of natural languages. I should add that I personally believe, and very many linguists share this belief, that, even if the attempt he has made to formalize the concepts employed in the analysis of languages should fail, the attempt itself will have immeasurably increased our understanding of these concepts and that in this respect the "Chomskyan revolution" cannot but be successful.

Formal Languages
and Formal Grammars

The purpose of this appendix is to provide, for students
of linguistics and others who are interested in such
questions, a rather more technical account of the basic
concepts of Chomskyan generative grammar than I have
thought proper to include in the main body of the
book. Many of the terms defined below—"sentence,"
"language," "grammar," "rule," and so on—are employed freely in the preceding chapters, where I have
not been as careful as I shall be here to establish and
maintain a distinction between formal languages and
natural languages. In what follows we shall be concerned primarily with formal languages, and the term
"language" will be defined in such a way that whatever
satisfies the definition will count as a formal language.

The relationship between formal languages and
natural languages (such as English, Turkish, Chinese,
and Swahili) is a matter of controversy among linguists. The view taken here is that, whether natural
languages are or are not formal languages, they have

certain properties (duality of structure, recursivity, grammatical ambiguity, and so on) that they share with particular kinds of formal languages. Insofar as natural languages and formal languages share the same structural properties, formal languages may usefully serve as *models* of natural languages. It is important to realize, however, that the notion of a formal language is totally independent, in principle, of the notion of a natural language. It is also, as we shall see, a much more general notion. Such terms as "sentence" and "vocabulary," which I use in my definition of "language," must be understood to have as general a sense as the definitions in which they occur allow them to have.

I begin by defining a *language* (that is, a formal language) as a set of sentences and a *sentence* as a finite sequence, or *string*, of elements, each of which is drawn from a finite *vocabulary*. More precisely, we can say that sentences consist of *tokens* of the elements that exist as *types* in the vocabulary. For example, given that the vocabulary, V, of the language, L, is the two-member set $\{a, b\}$, L might have as its members not only a, b, ab, and ba but also aa, aba, bba, and so on. The strings aa and aba each contain two tokens of the same type, a; the string bba contains two tokens of the type b; and so on. For the moment, we will simply take for granted this notion of type-token identity, in terms of which we can say that several tokens, or instances, of the same element can occur in several different strings or at several different places in the same string, although the vocabulary from which the elements are drawn contains only one element of the type in question. If σ (sigma) is a string of tokens whose types are contained in V, then σ is said to be a string *over* V. Any set of strings over V is a language over V.

The *length* of a string is determined by the number of elements (that is, element tokens) of which it is composed. For example, given that $V = \{a, b\}$, *aa* is a string of length 2 over V, *bab* is a string of length 3 over V, and so on. Strings may be finite or infinite in length; but sentences, as we have seen, are defined as of finite length. Not only sequences of two or more elements but also single elements are said to be strings; they are strings of length 1. We shall also introduce as a member of every set of strings over any vocabulary the *empty string*, or *null string*, which we will symbolize as 0 (zero) and define to be of length zero. All strings other than the empty string are *non-null*.

In saying that strings are sequences, rather than sets, of elements, we imply that they have the property of *linearity*—that each of the elements in a string occupies a particular position (and no two elements occupy the same position). In all strings of whatever length, there will be one (and only one) element that is the successor of no other element, and this we take to be the first element in the string. The position of all other elements (in strings of length i, where $i \geqq 2$) may be defined in terms of the relation of succession: The second element is the element that immediately follows the first, and in general the $n + 1$th element is the one that immediately follows the nth element in the string. All finite strings will have not only a first element but also a last element, definable as the element that has no successor. (In strings of length 1 the last element will, of course, be identical with the first element. We need not go into the question of how the notion of being the first or last element in the string applies to the empty string.) Two strings are *identical* if and only if they consist of exactly the same elements in exactly the same order.

Strings are formed by means of the binary operation of *concatenation*. Using the Greek letters ϕ, χ, and ψ as variables, we can say then $\phi^\frown\chi$ (i.e., the result of concatenating ϕ and χ) is also a string. Concatenation, like ordinary arithmetical addition, is *associative*:

$(\phi^\frown\chi)^\frown\psi = \phi^\frown(\chi^\frown\psi)$. Unlike the operation of addition, however, it is *noncommutative*: $\phi^\frown\chi \neq \chi^\frown\phi$. The empty string serves as an identity element with respect to concatenation (as zero serves as an identity-element with respect to ordinary arithmetical addition): thus $\phi^\frown o = o^\frown\phi = \phi$. Given that V is a finite vocabulary and that V* is the set of all finite strings over V, V* is *closed* under the operation of concatenation, in the sense that, if ϕ and χ are in the set U, then $\phi^\frown\chi$ is also in V*.

If there are m elements in the vocabulary—i.e., V = $\{v_1, v_2, v_3, \ldots, V_m\}$—there will be exactly m strings of length 1 in V*, m^2 strings of length 2, and in general m^i strings of length i. The set of all strings of length i over V may be referred to as V^i. Thus: V^0 will be the one-member set of strings of length zero; V^1 will be the m-member set of strings of length 1; V^2 will be the m^2-member set of strings of length 2; and so on. V* will therefore be the *union* of all V^i: $V^* = V^0 + V^1 + V^2 + \ldots$. If V is finite and no upper bound is set to i, there will be an infinite (but *denumerably infinite*) number of strings in V*. (To say of any set that it is *denumerable* is to say that its members can be put into correspondence with the natural numbers $\{1, 2, 3, \ldots\}$. There are higher orders of infinity than denumerable infinity.)

Every finite or infinite subset of V* is a language (and there is a nondenumerable infinity of them). Using the letter L to refer to the set of all languages over V (i.e., to all of the subsets of V*), we can distinguish one member of L from another by means of a nonnumerical subscript. Thus: L = $\{L_a, L_b, L_c, \ldots\}$. (These nonnumerical subscripts, it should be noted, are to be distinguished, in terms of their function, from the numerical superscripts introduced above to refer to sets of strings of a particular length. V^0, V^1, V^2, etc. are members of L, since they are all subsets of V*; but there are infinitely many members of L_a, L_b, L_c,

. . . that are not members of $\{V^0, V^1, V^2, \ldots\}$. Any string in L_x (where L_x is some arbitrary member of L) is a sentence of L_x: It is a grammatically *well-formed* string; it has the property of *grammaticality*. Any string over V that is not a string in L_x is *ill-formed*, or *ungrammatical*, with respect to L_x, although it may very well be a grammatical sentence of some other arbitrary language over V—of L_y, let us say. It follows that every sentence of L_x or L_y is grammatical in L_x or L_y, respectively.

Any finite specification of the sentences of L_x (i.e., any device, or set of rules, for determining the membership of L_x) is a grammar of L_x: It *generates* L_x. Some languages, if not all, are such that they are generated by more than one grammar. We will use the expression $G(L_x)$ to refer to the set of all the grammars that generate L_x. If $G(L_x)$ contains more than one member, we can distinguish them, one from another, by means of arbitrary numerical subscripts: $G_1(L_x)$, $G_2(L_x)$, etc. (The use of numerical subscripts is not to be understood as implying that the grammars of a language can be ordered, by whatever principle, in a series. As we shall see presently, there is at least a partial hierarchical ordering among grammars based on their relative power.) Any two (or more) grammars that generate the same language, e.g., L_x, are said to be (*weakly*) *equivalent*. Given that $G_1(L_x)$ and $G_2(L_x)$ are equivalent (in this sense of equivalence), but not identical, we can ask what are the formal properties that differentiate them.

Some formal languages are more interesting than others—both intrinsically, in some intuitively clear sense, and as potential models for the description of natural languages. If L_x is finite, it will always be possible in principle to specify the sentences of L_x by listing them, i.e., by constructing what may be referred to as a *list grammar*. If L_x is an infinite language, it will be impossible to specify its sentences by listing them. List grammars are intrinsically uninteresting. Furthermore, they are uninteresting as models for the description of natural languages, which, whether they are infinite or not (see Chapter v), are certainly not learned as lists of sentences by native speakers. Many of the languages that can be specified by the list grammars can be specified by intrinsically more interesting grammars. But any language that cannot be specified otherwise than by listing the sentences that it contains is, for our purposes at least, by virtue of that very fact, uninteresting.

Hardly more interesting than the languages generated by list grammars are the members of V'. As far as we know, there is no natural language whose sentences are all strings of length 2, or of length 7, or of length 109, or of any fixed length. But even if all the sentences of some natural language are strings of fixed length, we can be sure that their length will not be the only property that distinguishes them from nonsentences (i.e., ungrammatical strings over the same vocabulary). All sentences might be of length 6, but not all strings of length 6 will be sentences.

Without going farther into this question, let us simply say that of the indefinitely many languages over any finite vocabulary V some, but not others, will be intrinsically interesting in terms of their formal properties; and that of those that are intrinsically interesting some, but not others, will be interesting as models for the description of natural languages— namely, subsets of V* (given that V is of the same order of magnitude as are the vocabularies of natural language) that have at least some of the same formal properties as English, Turkish, Chinese, Swahili, and other natural languages. We will concentrate, therefore, as Chomsky did in his early work, on particular subclasses of formal languages; and we will talk about them, and about the grammars that generate them, within the same theoretical and terminological framework that Chomsky used.

The most powerful type of formal grammar is what is called an *unrestricted rewriting system*—a system of rules each of which has the form $\phi \to \chi$ ("rewrite ϕ as χ") with no restrictions imposed on the values of the variables ϕ and χ. This is more powerful than various kinds of *restricted rewriting systems* in that there are certain kinds of languages that are generated by unrestricted writing systems (over a given vocabulary V) but are not generated by restricted rewriting systems (over the same vocabulary V). It has been shown by Chomsky and others that within the class of restricted rewriting systems there are some that are more powerful than others. It has been shown, in fact, that within the class of grammars formalized as rewriting systems there is a hierarchy with at least four levels. At the top of this hierarchy are unrestricted rewriting systems—grammars of Type 0; at the bottom (less powerful grammars than this being of no interest as potential models of natural languages) we have finite-state grammars (informally discussed in Chapter v)—grammars of Type 4. The languages generated by Type 4 grammars are known, for historically irrelevant reasons, as *regular languages.* (The term is unfortunate in that it can be easily misunderstood as implying that only regular languages are subject to rule.) The general principle governing the hierarchical classification of grammars in terms of their power is that of inclusion as a relation holding between the languages generated by the grammars in question. That is to say: The languages generated by grammars of Type 4 are properly included as a subclass of the languages generated by grammars of Type 3; the languages generated by grammars of Type 3 are properly included in the languages generated by grammars of Type 2; and, in general, the languages generated by grammars of Type i are also generated by grammars of Type $i - 1$, but not the reverse. Grammars of Type 3 include *context-free phrase structure* (CF) grammars, and grammars of Type 2 include *context-sensitive phrase structure* (CS) grammars. The languages generated by Type 3 and Type 2 grammars, respectively, may be referred to as CF languages and CS languages (or, more fully, as context-free languages and context-sensitive languages). The languages generated by Type 1 grammars are known as *recursive* languages, and they constitute a proper subset of *recursively enumerable* languages, which are generated by Type 0 grammars.

The difference between recursive sets and recursively enumerable sets, upon which the difference between the languages generated by Type 1 and Type 0 grammars ultimately depends, is one whose mathematical implications need not concern us. (A recursive set is a recursively enumerable set whose complement is also recursively enumerable.) The important point is that there is an identifiable class of formal languages that properly includes CS languages and is properly included in the class of recursively enumerable languages. The question for the theoretical linguist is whether formal grammars of one type rather than another will serve best as models for the description of natural languages. As we have seen in the main body of the book, Chomsky has argued strongly for the view that it is impossible, in principle, to describe the syntax of natural languages by means of a grammar that is less powerful than a CF grammar (Type 3).

The CF grammars differ from the more powerful class of CS grammars (Type 2) in that the latter, but not the former, permit the use of context-sensitive rules, i.e., rules of the form

$$\phi \rightarrow \chi \;/\; \alpha - \beta$$

("ϕ is rewritten as χ in the environment of a preceding α and a following β") where ϕ, χ, α, and β are all variables ranging over strings. Both CF grammars and CS grammars make use of the distinction between *auxiliary symbols* and *terminal symbols*. We can make this distinction apparent, notationally, by using capital italic letters, $\{A, B, C, \ldots\}$, for the former, and small italic letters, $\{a, b, c, \ldots\}$, for the latter. For example, the rule

$$A \to a \, / \, B \, \text{—} \, C$$

would be interpreted to mean that the auxiliary symbol A is replaced by the terminal symbol a when, in the string to which the rule is applied, A is preceded by B and followed by C. The CF grammars are, of course, a proper subclass of CS grammars in that a context-free rule is but the special case of a context-sensitive rule in which no specific values are assigned to the contextual variables α and β.

The rules of both CF grammars and CS grammars are subject to certain restrictions. Neither ϕ nor χ can be the identity element (i.e., the empty string); ϕ cannot be a terminal symbol; ϕ cannot be a string containing more than a single symbol; and χ cannot (properly or improperly) include ϕ as a *substring*. Both CF grammars and CS grammars are *phrase structure* (PS) grammars; and, as we saw in Chapter vi, they (associated with certain conventions) not only generate strings of terminal symbols, *terminal strings*, but assign to each such terminal string a particular kind of *structural description*—an analysis of the terminal string in terms of a *labeled bracketing*. To assign such a structural description to the terminal strings that they generate is the function of the auxiliary, or nonterminal, symbols. The effect of the restrictions listed at the beginning of this paragraph is to reduce considerably the power of the class of grammars that the restrictions, in part, define. For example, it can be proved that a phrase structure grammar with deletion rules (i.e., rules of the form $\phi \to o$) has the power of an unrestricted rewriting system. Taken together (and formulated rather more precisely than I have done here), the restrictions listed above also ensure that each terminal string has a determinable structural description.

The PS grammars, as we saw in Chapter vi, consist of sets of rules (each of the form $\phi \to \chi \ / \ \alpha - \beta$). The rules can be *ordered* or *unordered*. If they are unordered, any rule that is applicable to a string (by virtue of the occurrence in that string of a symbol corresponding to the symbol on the left-hand side of rule) may be applied to the string in question, regardless of whether some other rule in the set has been applied (if applicable) or not. If they are ordered, a rule that is ordered later in the set cannot be applied before a rule that is ordered earlier in the set has been applied (if it is applicable). The question of rule ordering is important because the set of languages that is generated by ordered PS grammars is not identical with the set of languages generated by unordered PS grammars. The sample CF grammar given in Chapter vi was unordered.

But the particular *derivation* that was referred to in the discussion of the sample CF grammar in Chapter vi was different from alternative derivations of the same terminal string; and, if the reader works carefully through some alternative derivations, he will see that the derivations differ (when they differ) by virtue of a difference in the order in which the rules are applied. This does not mean that the grammar is ordered in the same sense in which the term "ordered" is being used here. There is some degree of *intrinsic ordering*: (iv) cannot apply unless (ii) has applied; (vi) cannot apply unless (iii) has applied; and so on. But there is no *extrinsic ordering*, and this is what is usually meant when the term "ordering" is used in the classification of grammars. A distinction must be drawn between the ordering of rules in the grammar and the order in which they are applied in a given derivation. As far as the sample grammar of Chapter vi is concerned, and this holds true of all CF grammars that are subject to the restrictions listed earlier, the *phrase markers* (i.e., the structural descriptions assigned by a grammar to the terminal strings that it generates) are to be identified not with particular derivations but with equivalence classes of alternative derivations.

Given that the vocabulary of a particular PS grammar includes both a set of nonterminal (or auxiliary) symbols, $V_N = \{A, B, C, \ldots\}$, and a set of terminal symbols, $V_T = \{a, b, c, \ldots\}$, such that V is the union of V_N and V_T (i.e., $V = V_N + V_T$), we can see that a derivation will be a sequence of strings over V, each string in the sequence being *derived* from its predecessor in the sequence by some rule in the grammar. The first member in a sequence has no predecessor; the *initial string* of a derivation cannot therefore be formed, by a rule $\phi \rightarrow \chi \, / \, \alpha - \beta$, from some preceding string in the derivation. Our PS grammar will have associated with it a statement telling us what members of V* are to count as initial strings: e.g., $\Sigma = \{Ba, bCc, \ldots\}$, where Σ is the set of initial strings. The initial strings are, as it were, the *axioms*; and each string that can be derived from one of the initial strings by the application of one or more rules is comparable with a theorem provable in a formal system. The last member of any derivation will be a string over V_T, i.e., a string consisting of only terminal symbols. A PS grammar will generate, therefore, both terminal strings (a subset of the strings over V_T) and nonterminal strings (a subset of the strings over V containing at least one element from V_N). By our definitions of "language" and "sentence" both terminal and nonterminal strings are sentences of the language generated by a PS grammar. In using PS grammars as models for the description of natural languages, we can readily restrict the definition of "sentence" so that only terminal strings will be recognized as sentences.

I have deliberately chosen as examples of initial strings, or axioms, strings from V* that contain both terminal and nonterminal symbols: *Ba* and *bCc*. There must be at least one nonterminal symbol in any initial string that serves as the first member of a derivation. It is important to realize, however, that the initial strings are not necessarily single elements, i.e., members of V_N. The initial string in Chapter vi was the symbol *Sentence*; but no explicit statement, $\Sigma = \{Sentence, \ldots\}$, was made to this effect. Generally speaking, in the applications that linguists have made of PS grammars, they have explicitly or implicitly restricted the set of initial strings to one-member sets containing some particular member of V_N. By convention, the symbol *S* (in works written in English) is usually reserved for this purpose; and this symbol may be thought of as being mnemonically connected with the term "sentence."

One other symbol must now be mentioned: the *boundary symbol*, #. If we add to V the symbol # and then, whether by rule or convention, ensure that the initial string contains as both the first and the last element in the string a token of #, we shall be able to write context-sensitive rules of the form

$$\phi \rightarrow \chi \ / \ \#\alpha - \beta$$

or

$$\phi \rightarrow \chi \ / \ \alpha - \beta\#$$

(where, as always, α and β may be either null or non-null), in order to indicate that ϕ must occur at the beginning or end of a string or, more generally, at some specified number of positions from the beginning or end of the string.

Given that the initial string is $\#^\frown S^\frown \#$ and, further, that no other boundary symbols are introduced into the strings generated by the grammar, every terminal string will contain just two tokens of #, one as the first and one as the last element of the string. (In view of our earlier definition of "terminal string," it now follows that, if the boundary symbols are to count as elements in terminal strings, # must be added to V_T. But this is a technicality of relatively minor importance. All that was said earlier was that # is a member of V.) Let us suppose, however that our grammar contains rules of the form

$$\phi \rightarrow \chi \frown \# \frown S \frown \# \frown \psi \: / \: \alpha - \beta$$

i.e., rules that introduce tokens of the initial string into strings derived by other rules from the initial string. First of all, it will be observed, such rules are *recursive*; and, as we saw in Chapter v, there is reason to believe that any formal grammar that is to serve as a model for the description of a natural language must contain at least one recursive rule. This does not mean, of course, that the recursive rule (or rules) that appears in the grammar must necessarily have on the right-hand side of the arrow an instance of the initial string. But Chomsky has consistently held to the view that there is no subsentential recursion in natural languages.

Furthermore, in an *Aspects*-type transformational grammar, it is not just S but also $\# \frown S \frown \#$ that is *embedded* by means of the recursive rules of the base component. (See Chapter vi.) The string-internal boundary symbols are then erased by means of a convention associated with the operation of certain *cyclical* transformations (provided that these rules, which are extrinsically ordered, have been applied in the proper order). It thus becomes possible to use the presence or absence of sentence-internal boundary symbols in strings (or, more generally, in phrase markers) to *filter* out a certain class of ill-formed surface structures. The importance of this rather technical point (which cannot be developed in full here) derives from the fact that filtering of the kind that an *Aspects*-type grammar permits has now been shown to increase the power of a transformational grammar to the point where transformational grammars that have this property and are otherwise unconstrained are weakly equivalent to Type o grammars. It is generally agreed that any formal grammar that is as powerful as this is far too powerful as a model for the description of natural languages. As I pointed out in Chapter vii, current work in the development of Chomskyan transformational grammars is directed toward an empirically motivated reduction of their power.

No more will be said here about the technicalities of transformational grammars. All the general points that need to be made about formal grammars as models for the description of natural languages can be made with reference, in the first instance, to PS grammars. It suffices to remind the reader that the formalization of transformational grammars and the investigation of the properties of the languages that they generate (on the assumption that the grammars in question are so constrained that they generate a proper subset of the recursively enumerable languages over some large, but finite, vocabulary V) is far more complex than the formalization of PS grammars and, especially, CF languages, which are now well understood.

One important distinction that can now be drawn is the distinction between *weak equivalence* and *strong equivalence*. As we have seen, two grammars, $G_i(L_x)$ and $G_j(L_y)$, are weakly equivalent if and only if they both generate exactly the same language; and $L_x = L_y$, it will be recalled, if and only if they both contain exactly the same set of terminal strings over a common vocabulary V_T. (I adjusted the definition of weak equivalence to take account of the distinction, subsequently introduced, of terminal and nonterminal strings. The sentences of L_x and L_y are now the terminal strings generated by grammars of L_x and L_y.) Two grammars, $G_i(L_x)$ and $G_j(L_y)$, are strongly equivalent if and only if they generate the same *structures*. To illustrate: The structures generated by PS grammars are phrase markers (i.e., labeled bracketings). Two PS grammars will, therefore, be strongly equivalent if and only if they both generate the same phrase markers. A terminal string is a part of every well-formed phrase marker in the set of phrase markers (over the terminal and nonterminal vocabulary) generated by a grammar, and a phrase marker may be regarded as a structural description of the terminal string that it contains. What has just been said can, therefore, be understood to imply that two grammars are strongly equivalent if they not only generate the same sentences but also assign to each sentence the same set of structural descriptions. As far as PS grammars are concerned, they will be strongly non-equivalent if the structures that they generate differ with respect to either the labeling or the bracketing (or both). As we saw in Chapter vi, the fact that different labeled bracketings can be assigned to the same terminal string means that one kind of *structural ambiguity* that is found in natural languages is readily identifiable (under a certain interpretation of the correspondence that holds between formal and natural languages) with one of the properties of CF languages and CS languages.

Other kinds of formal grammars—notably *categorial grammars* and *dependency grammars*—have been proved to be at least weakly, and perhaps strongly, equivalent to PS grammars. The reason why I say "perhaps" is that, when it comes to the consideration of what are taken to be comparable structures, it is not always clear what counts as a significant difference and what is no more than *notational variation*. Both categorial grammars and dependency grammars assign to the strings that they generate structures that can be treated as labeled bracketings. To this extent, therefore, a given categorial grammar or a given dependency grammar might be held to be strongly equivalent to a given PS grammar. It can be argued, however, that, insofar as the nonterminal vocabulary of a categorial grammar consists of both basic and derived categories and the principle whereby the derived categories are constructed out of basic categories directly reflects the distribution and syntactic function of each derived category, the labels are more than simply notational variants of the nonterminal symbols, {*A*, *B*, *C*, . . .}, in a PS grammar. Categorial grammars have been mentioned here (though not explained) because they play an important role in certain current alternatives to Chomsky's own system of transformational-generative grammar. (See Chapter viii.)

We turn now to a brief consideration of the question of relating formal languages to natural languages by taking the former (or a subclass of the former) as *models* of the latter. The term "model" has several senses. In the sense in which it is being used here, a model is a deliberately restricted and abstract representation of the phenomena whose structure or behavior is being investigated. The construction of such models by the physicist, the economist, or the linguist necessarily involves some degree of idealization. If the model is to have any explanatory value or predictive power, however, it must contain elements and relations that can be put into *correspondence* with elements and relations of the system that is being modeled.

So far we have talked of natural languages rather than of natural language. We will proceed on the working assumption that all natural languages share certain properties, such that it is reasonable to expect that their grammatical structures will be describable in terms of formal grammars of the same general type and the same power. This, as we have seen, is an assumption that Chomsky makes. Indeed, the way in which he formulates that assumption and makes it mathematically precise is an essential part of the "Chomskyan revolution," independent of the philosophical and psychological conclusions that he draws from it. (See Chapter xi.)

The natural-language correlates of the well-formed terminal strings of a formal language are, of course, sentences. But what are the natural-language correlates of the members of V_T?

All known natural languages have at least two *levels* of structure: the phonological and the syntactic. (See Chapter ii.) The lower-level units are *phonemes*; the higher-level units are *forms* (of which words— more precisely, word forms—are a subclass). Forms are composed of phonemes; but the distribution of a form is, in general, not predictable in terms of its phonological composition. Minimal forms are *morphemes* (under one interpretation of the term "morpheme"). It might seem reasonable, therefore, to take the natural-language correlates of the members of V_T— the syntactic *primes* of natural languages—to be morphemes. Several problems arise immediately.

1. In all natural languages, utterances differ from one another significantly, not only in terms of the forms of which they are composed but also in terms of their *prosodic contour* (i.e., stress pattern and intonation pattern). It is pretheoretically unclear how much of this systematic prosodic variation is to be treated as being part of the sentence, but some of it would normally be so treated by linguists. This means that natural-language sentences are not just strings of morphemes. In order to put natural-language sentences into correspondence with the terminal strings of some concatenating formal language, we must represent

what is essentially nonlinear by means of elements that, whether arbitrarily or not, are given a certain position in a string of morpheme correlates.

2. In all natural languages, there is a greater or lesser degree of homonymy; that is, a single form may have two different (and unrelated) meanings (for example, *bank* in English). More important than the difference in meaning, in the present connection, is the fact that the same form may belong to several different syntactic classes (for example, *down* in English). Do we correlate a single natural-language form with several formal-language elements? The answer is pretheoretically unclear, and no clear and unequivocal answer is provided by current linguistic theory.

3. More serious is the fact that morphemes (in the sense of minimal forms) are not as readily identifiable in certain natural languages (such as Latin) as they are, generally speaking, in English. It is arguable that the sentences of such languages do not consist of strings of morphemes and that, by putting them into correspondence with the terminal strings of a concatenating formal language (that is, in a one-to-one, morpheme-to-element, order-preserving correspondence), we necessarily introduce so high a degree of arbitrariness as to constitute distortion.

There are problems, then, with the assumption that morphemes are, in all natural languages, the correlates of formal-language elements on the syntactic level of representation. These problems can always be solved at the price of arbitrariness or, alternatively, by postulating the existence of rather more abstract forms and complicating the relationship between the phonological and the syntactic level (as this is represented in the model). It may well be that there are empirically valid, and discoverable, reasons for postulating the existence of more abstract minimal forms. We will

not go into this question. The point being made here
is that, in some, if not all, natural languages, the
relationship between syntax and phonology is far more
complex than the simplest statement of the principle
of duality, in terms of phonemes and morphemes,
might suggest.

And it is not just a matter of relating the two levels
of syntax and phonology in our models of natural
languages. Whether there should be sublevels within
phonology (sublevels at which such units as syllables
and phonological words are identified) is perhaps debatable. There can be no question but that there are
various sublevels to be recognized within syntax. The
most obvious of these is the sublevel whose primes are
words (or, more precisely, word forms). In some languages, words are readily identifiable as strings of
morphemes; in other languages, they are not. In some
languages, word order plays a significant grammatical
role; in others, its function is stylistic rather than
grammatical. Once again, we have what appears to
be important structural differences among natural
languages. It is arguable that our models should
directly reflect such differences. Formal languages of
the kind that we have been considering in this appendix
are, by definition, sets of strings over vocabularies of
elements, or primes. But a case can be made for the
view that, in some natural languages at least, sequen-
tial position plays no part at all at the higher sublevels
of syntax (the sublevels of words and phrases). This
point is controversial and will not be pressed. It is but
one of several that could be made to emphasize the
complexity and diversity of the formal structures that
we find in natural languages.

The reader will have noted that there is nothing in
the definition of formal languages to say that the elements in their vocabularies or the strings of elements
that constitute their sentences should be meaningful.
Indeed, nothing in the definition of "language" refers

to communication or any particular function of the system whose grammatical structure we may be studying. Formal languages may be treated either as *interpreted* or *uninterpreted* systems. There are various ways in which a *semantic interpretation* can be assigned to the elements and sentences of a formal language. We need not go into this. It is important to realize, however, that the syntax of a formal language is describable without reference to any interpretation that might be assigned to the elements or combinations of elements; and a formal language might serve as a model, in principle, for all sorts of systems that have nothing to do with communication and would never be described as languages in the everyday sense of the term. The goal of theoretical linguistics can be described as that of constructing a class of formal languages, all of whose members share certain general properties and each of whose members can be put into correspondence with some actual or potential natural language. It is as yet unclear whether this goal can be achieved.

Since the appearance of the first edition of this book,
The Logical Structure of Linguistic Theory (hereafter
abbreviated as *LSLT*) was published and in it an Introduction, dated 1973, in which Chomsky explains
the "rather unusual status" of his manuscript and
sets it in its historical context. He points out that,
apart from the original 1955 version (which was left
unfinished), there is a partially edited and revised
version from January 1956. Of these versions, the first
was both duplicated and microfilmed and the second
was microfilmed. In 1956, Chomsky began to revise
the manuscript for publication, but he abandoned this
task when the MIT Press, to which he submitted parts
of the manuscript, rejected it "with the not unreason-
able observation that an unknown author taking a
rather unconventional approach should submit articles
based on this material to professional journals before
planning to publish such a comprehensive and detailed
manuscript as a book." The one article on generative

grammars that Chomsky had submitted to a linguistics journal "had been rejected, virtually by return mail" and, as far as he could determine while lecturing at various universities, "there was little interest in these topics among professional linguists."

It was at the suggestion of Morris Halle, to whom he showed some of his "lecture notes for an undergraduate course at MIT," that he approached the editor of Mouton's *Janua Linguarum* series. What subsequently appeared as *Syntactic Structures* was a "slightly revised version" of the lecture notes, containing "a sketchy and informal outline of some of the material in *LSLT*, along with some material on finite-state grammars and formal properties of grammars from 1956."

What Chomsky has to say here about the origin of *Syntactic Structures* and the unpublishability of *LSLT* should be read by anyone who has access to the now published version of *LSLT* and is puzzled by my footnote on page 67 of Chapter vi above. Chomsky also explains in his Introduction to the 1975 version of *LSLT* that his adoption of the "methodological," rather than the "psychological," interpretation of the linguist's task was determined by his feeling that it would have been "too audacious" for him to have raised the issue of justifying grammars in psychological terms at that time. As he points out, R. B. Lees did raise this issue in his provocative, but influential, 1957 review of *Syntactic Structures* in *Language* magazine. Chomsky says that "the 'psychological analogue' to the methodological problems of constructing linguistic theory," though not discussed in *LSLT*, "lay in the immediate background" of his thinking; and, in preparing *LSLT* for publication a second time in 1958–59 (a task that was, once again, abandoned, owing to the pressure of other commitments), he presented the alternative psychological interpretation "as the framework for the entire study." He has continued to do

so ever since. (The 1975 published version of *LSLT*
is an amalgam based on the 1955 version and the
two 1956 versions. It does not contain anything from
the 1958–59 revision and, thus, sets generative grammar within the earlier nonpsychological framework.)

Chomsky's Introduction in *LSLT* contains much that
is of historical importance. But there is nothing else,
I think, that would lead me to revise my classification
of his early work as being essentially "Bloomfieldian"
in spirit. It now appears, however, that it was deliberately given this character by Chomsky. It was
Syntactic Structures that first made Chomsky's ideas
known to linguists. If this, being deliberately "watered
down," was interpreted differently by different groups
of linguists, it is hardly surprising. I, for one, thought
that Lees, in his review, read into it much that was
not there. On the other hand, by virtue of my own
background, I immediately related Chomsky's notion
of generative grammar to the ideas of Saussure and
Humboldt, whereas it was only much later that Chomsky himself became aware of the connection.

In his detailed and informative review of the first
edition of the present work, Dell Hymes criticizes many
aspects of both my account of the context and development of Chomsky's work and my assessment of
Chomsky as an intellectual figure. I cannot comment
here upon all the points he makes, but I shall mention
the most important and give some indication of my
response. (For Hymes's review, see the "Short Bibliography," which follows this appendix. Page references
are to the reprint version.)

Hymes suggests, as many have done, that in my
presentation of Chomsky's early work I exaggerated
its "Bloomfieldian" character (pages 324–27). If this
is so, the reason, as will now be clear, is that Chomsky
himself deliberately suppressed in publication what
would have been, in 1957, an excessively "non-Bloomfieldian" appeal to the native speaker's intuitions, to

the "psychological analogue," and to the integration of
syntax with semantics. Hymes had the advantage of
being present, at the time, at conferences and meetings
at which it became clear earlier than it did in published work that Chomsky was less of a "Bloomfieldian"
than he appears to be as he presents himself in
Syntactic Structures. I concede, therefore, that the
view that I gave of Chomsky's early work was perhaps
limited by the fact that I (like most non-American
linguists) knew nothing of the "non-Bloomfieldian"
element in Chomsky's thought until much later. Indeed, I cannot now recall being made aware of this
during the year 1960–61, which I spent in the United
States (though not in direct contact with Chomsky).
But by then I had long been fixed in my own opinion
of Chomsky's theory of grammar, and I may simply
have assumed that it was shared by others. However
that may be, I hope that Hymes is wrong when he says
that, in my account of Chomsky's early work, I was
guilty of a "soft-pedaling, to the point of inaudibility,
of any note of the dramatic impact" that this had at
the time. The impact of Chomsky's work on my thinking and on that of other linguists with whom I was
discussing it in 1957 was certainly dramatic enough,
and I am sorry if this did not come out clearly in
my book.

Hymes takes me to task for saying that there has
never been a "Sapirian" school of linguistics. He
submits "that in the 1930's there was at the very least
a Sapir tradition, and a group of younger scholars
whose work was thoroughly informed by it" (page
321). I accept this point entirely—the more readily as
Hymes himself is probably the most eminent living
representative of that tradition—but there is a difference between a "school" and a "tradition," and we are
both agreed that there was never a "Sapirian" ortho-
doxy. What Hymes makes clear in his review (and I

did not in Chapter iii) is that the "Bloomfieldian" school was largely the creation not of Bloomfield himself but of a group of men "who took a certain conception of Bloomfield as its symbol." As he suggests, the climate of American linguistics might have been very different if Sapir had not died in 1939. There is much else in Hymes's discussion of my account of American linguistics in the pre-Chomskyan period (notably his comments on the role of Boas and his suggestion that the appeal of "various forms of operationalism, positivism, and behaviorism, at least as a style and ideology" had a great deal to do with the "skepticism and even cynicism as to traditional concepts and rationalism in all fields" [page 320] in the period after World War I) that I cannot deal with here. What Hymes has to say is extremely interesting, and I refer the reader to the review itself and to other works of his own that Hymes cites therein.

I accept that "it is ideological confidence rather than empirical knowledge" (page 318) that leads me and other linguists to say (as I do in Chapter ii) that all languages are "of roughly equal complexity." I also accept that "to say that every language has sufficiently rich vocabulary for the expression of all the distinctions that are important in the society using it is to beg a host of questions" (page 317). Whether it is true that this brand of "functional optimism" (which Hymes attributes to the uncritical acceptance by "most linguists" of "a liberal humanist ideology formed earlier in the century" [page 318]) "would not pass muster for a moment in the political circles in which Chomsky figures" (page 317), I do not know. But I still believe that, until we have more evidence than there is at present to decide the issue otherwise, it is preferable for the linguist to emphasize, as I have done, the fact that no language is more "primitive" than any other. Nonetheless, I agree with Hymes that one should try to study, empirically and without ideological prejudice, the possibility of there being some kind of correlation between language and culture.

The most serious criticism that Hymes makes of my book is that, in not dealing with Chomsky as a political figure, I failed to show how "the impact of Chomsky, as of other men, has been jointly a product of the man, the work and the times" (page 323). I freely admit that this was a limitation of the book. I simply did not feel that I could do justice to Chomsky's political commitment. In his review, Hymes goes a long way toward compensating for this deficiency of my book. He talks of another kind of "Chomskyan revolution," different from the one to which I referred in the final paragraph of my book—a revolution that has as its goal "the realization of human values"—and describes Chomsky as "a dramatically successful scholar who would put his mind and to some extent his body on the line for causes that matter—a man who publicly and committedly broke with the age-old tradition of *trahison des clercs*" (page 329). This is indeed a very important element in the impact that Chomsky made in the 1960s and early 1970s. How lasting this impact will be I do not know. "Perhaps," as Hymes puts it in his final sentence, "one must always wait a generation, for memoirs, retrospection and the like, before the owl of Minerva can take her flight."

In conclusion, I would draw attention to Hymes's suggestion that, "if Chomsky established grammaticality as an effective criterion, as against occurrence in a corpus, the next step in linguistics would appear to be to establish appropriateness and acceptability." As I explain in the final chapter of the present edition, there has recently been a noticeable shift of interest, within linguistics, toward the social and the behavioral. I should mention here that Hymes has played a major role in bringing this about. Although I do not myself consider that there is, as yet, any good reason to abandon the Chomskyan idealization of linguistic competence, I would agree with Hymes that language should also be studied as human activity, within a framework to which ethnography and social psychology make an essential contribution. Hymes's *Foundations in Sociolinguistics* is an excellent starting point for anyone who wishes to pursue this approach.

SHORT BIBLIOGRAPHY

INDEX

SHORT BIBLIOGRAPHY

Selected Works by Chomsky

1951 "Morphophonemics of Modern Hebrew." Unpublished master's thesis, University of Pennsylvania.

1953 "Systems of Syntactic Analysis," in *Journal of Symbolic Logic* 18: 242–56.

1955 "Logical Syntax and Semantics: Their Linguistic Relevance," in *Language* 31: 36–45.

"The Logical Structure of Linguistic Theory." Mimeographed, MIT Library, Cambridge, Mass. (Rev. ed. with an important and informative Introduction, 1975. See below.)

"Transformational Analysis." Unpublished Ph.D. dissertation, University of Pennsylvania.

"Semantic Considerations in Grammar." Monograph No. 8, pp. 141–53. Washington, D.C.: Georgetown University Institute of Languages and Linguistics.

1956 "On Accent and Juncture in English," with M. Halle and F. Lukoff, in M. Halle, H. Lunt, and H. MacLean (eds.), *For Roman Jakobson*. The Hague: Mouton.

"Three Models for the Description of Language." *I.R.E. Transactions on Information Theory*, Vol.

IT–2: 113–24. Reprinted, with corrections, in
R. D. Luce, R. Bush, and E. Galanter (eds.), *Readings in Mathematical Psychology*, Vol. II. New
York: Wiley, 1963.

"Logical Structures in Language," in *American Documentation* 8: 284–91.

1957 *Syntactic Structures.* The Hague: Mouton.
Review of Hockett, *Manual of Phonology*, in *International Journal of American Linguistics* 23:
223–34.

Review of Jakobson and Halle, *Fundamentals of Language*, in *International Journal of American Linguistics* 23: 234–42.

1958 "Finite State Languages," with G. A. Miller, in
Information and Control 1: 91–112. Reprinted
in R. D. Luce, R. Bush, and E. Galanter (eds.)
Readings in Mathematical Psychology, Vol. II.
New York: Wiley, 1963.

Review of Belevitch, *Langage des Machines et Langage Humain*, in *Language* 34: 99–105.

1959 Review of Skinner, *Verbal Behavior*, in *Language*
35: 26–58. Reprinted in Fodor and Katz, *The Structure of Language.*

Review of Greenberg, *Essays in Linguistics*, in
Word 15: 202–18.

"On Certain Formal Properties of Grammars," in
Information and Control 2: 137–67. Reprinted
in R. D. Luce, R. Bush, and E. Galanter (eds.),
Readings in Mathematical Psychology, Vol. II.
New York: Wiley, 1963.

"A Note on Phrase Structure Grammars," in *Information and Control* 2: 393–95.

1960 "The Morphophonemics of English," with M.
Halle, in *RLE Quarterly Progress Report No. 58.*
Cambridge, Mass.: Massachusetts Institute of
Technology.

1961 "On the notion 'rule of grammar,'" in R. Jakobson (ed.), *Structure of Language and Its Mathematical Aspect.* Providence: American
Mathematical Society. Reprinted in Fodor and
Katz, *The Structure of Language.*

1962 "Explanatory Models in Linguistics," in E. Nagel,
P. Suppes, and A. Tarski (eds.), *Logic, Methodology and Philosophy of Science: Proceedings of the 1960 International Congress.* Stanford, Cal.:
Stanford University Press.

"Context-free Grammars and Pushdown Storage,"
in *RLE Quarterly Progress Report No. 65.* Cam-

bridge, Mass.: Massachusetts Institute of Technology.

"A Transformational Approach to Syntax," in A. A. Hill (ed.), *Proceedings of the 1958 Conference on Problems of Linguistic Analysis in English*. Austin, Tex. Reprinted in Fodor and Katz, *The Structure of Language*.

1963 "The Algebraic Theory of Context-free Languages," with M. P. Schutzenberger, in P. Braffort and D. Hirschbert (eds.), *Computer Programming and Formal Systems*. Amsterdam: North-Holland.

"Formal Properties of Grammars," in R. D. Luce, R. Bush, and E. Galanter (eds.), *Handbook of Mathematical Psychology*, Vol. II. New York: Wiley.

"Introduction to the Formal Analysis of Natural Languages," with G. A. Miller, in *ibid.*

"Finitary Models of Language Users," with G. A. Miller, in *ibid.*

1964 *Current Issues in Linguistic Theory*. The Hague: Mouton.

"Formal Discussion: The Development of Grammar in Child Language," in U. Bellugi and R. Brown (eds.), *The Acquisition of Language*. Monographs of the Society for Research in Child Development 29: 1. Lafayette, Ind.: Purdue University.

1965 "Some Controversial Questions in Phonological Theory," with M. Halle, in *Journal of Linguistics* 1: 97–136.

Aspects of the Theory of Syntax. Cambridge, Mass.: MIT Press.

1966 *Cartesian Linguistics*. New York: Harper & Row.

Topics in the Theory of Generative Grammar. The Hague: Mouton. Also in T. A. Sebeok (ed.), *Current Trends in Linguistics, Vol. III: Linguistic Theory*. The Hague: Mouton, 1966.

"The Current Scene in Linguistics: Present Directions," in *College English* 27: 587–95. Reprinted in D. A. Reibel and S. A. Schane (eds.), *Modern Studies in English*. Englewood Cliffs, N.J.: Prentice-Hall, 1969.

1967 "The Formal Nature of Language." Appendix to E. H. Lenneberg, *Biological Foundations of Language*. New York: Wiley. Reprinted in 1972 edition of *Language and Mind* (see below).

"Some General Properties of Phonological Rules," in *Language* 43: 102–128.

"The General Properties of Language," in P. L. Darley (ed.), *Brain Mechanisms Underlying Speech and Language* (proceedings of a conference held at Princeton, N.J., November 9–12, 1965). New York: Grune & Stratton.

1968 *The Sound Pattern of English*, with M. Halle. New York: Harper & Row.

Language and Mind. New York: Harcourt, Brace & World.

1969 "Linguistics and Philosophy," in S. Hook (ed.), *Language and Philosophy.* New York: New York University Press (New York University Institute of Philosophy Symposium). Reprinted in 1972 edition of *Language and Mind* (see below).

"Knowledge of Language" (excerpted from the first John Locke Lecture, Oxford University, April 29, 1969), in *Times Literary Supplement* (London), May 15, 1969.

"Form and Meaning in Natural Language," in J. D. Roslansky (ed.), *Communication.* Amsterdam: North-Holland.

"Quine's Empirical Assumptions," in D. Davidson and J. Hintikka (eds.), *Words and Objections.* Dordrecht, Netherlands: Reidel.

"Some Empirical Assumptions in Modern Philosophy of Language," in S. Morgenbesser *et al.* (eds.), *Philosophy, Science and Method.* New York: St. Martin's.

American Power and the New Mandarins. New York: Pantheon.

1970 "Remarks on Nominalisation," in R. Jacobs and P. Rosenbaum (eds.), *Readings in Transformational Grammar.* Waltham, Mass.: Blaisdell. Reprinted in Chomsky, *Studies on Semantics in Generative Grammar,* 1972 (see below).

"Phonology and Reading," in H. Levin and J. P. Williams (eds.), *Basic Studies in Reading.* New York: Basic Books.

"Problems of Explanation in Linguistics," in R. Borger and F. Cioffa (eds.), *Explanations in the Behavioural Sciences.* New York: Cambridge University Press.

"Deep Structure, Surface Structure and Semantic Interpretation," in R. Jakobson and S. Kawamoto (eds.), *Studies in General and Oriental Linguistics.* Tokyo: TEC Corporation for Language Research. Reprinted in Chomsky, *Studies on Semantics in Generative Grammar,* 1972 (see below).

"Some Observations on the Problems of Semantic Analysis in Natural Languages," in A. J. Greimas *et al., Sign, Language, Culture.* The Hague: Mouton.

At War with Asia: Essays on Indochina. New York: Random House.

1971 *Problems of Freedom and Knowledge.* New York: Pantheon. Reprinted 1972 as *Problems of Knowledge and Freedom.* New York: Random.

1972 *Language and Mind,* enlarged edition. New York: Harcourt Brace Jovanovich. (Page references in the text are to the first edition.)

Studies on Semantics in Generative Grammar. The Hague: Mouton.

"Some Empirical Issues in the Theory of Transformational Grammar," in S. Peters (ed.), *Goals of Linguistic Theory.* Englewood Cliffs, N.J.: Prentice-Hall. (Also in Chomsky, *Studies on Semantics in Generative Grammar,* 1972.)

1973 "Conditions on Transformations," in S. R. Anderson and P. Kiparsky (eds.), *Festschrift for Morris Halle.* New York: Holt, Rinehart & Winston.

For Reasons of State. New York: Pantheon.

The Backroom Boys. New York: Pantheon.

1974 "Dialogue with Noam Chomsky," in P. Parret (ed.), *Discussing Language.* The Hague: Mouton.

Peace in the Middle East? New York: Vintage.

"What the Linguist Is Talking About," with J. J. Katz, in *Journal of Philosophy* 71: 347–67.

"On Innateness," with J. J. Katz, in *Philosophical Review* 84: 347–67.

1975 "Knowledge of Language," in K. Gunderson and J. L. Maxwell (eds.), *Minnesota Studies in Philosophy of Science,* Vol. VI. Minneapolis: University of Minnesota Press.

"Questions of Form and Interpretation," in *Linguistic Analysis* 1: 75–109.

The Logical Structure of Linguistic Theory. New York: Plenum.

"Conditions on Rules of Grammar." Unpublished manuscript.

1976 *Reflections on Language.* New York: Pantheon.

Other Works

Aitchison, J. *The Articulate Mammal.* London: Hutchinson, 1976.

Akmajian, A., and Heny, F. *An Introduction to the Principles of Transformational Syntax.* Cambridge, Mass.: MIT Press, 1975.

Allen, J. P. B., and Van Buren, P. (eds.). *Chomsky: Selected Readings.* New York: Oxford University Press, 1971.

Bach, E. *Syntactic Theory.* New York: Holt, Rinehart & Winston, 1974.

Bloomfield, L. *Language.* New York: Holt, Rinehart & Winston, 1933.

Boas, F. *Handbook of American Indian Languages.* Washington, D.C.: Smithsonian Institution, 1911.

Bolinger, D. *Aspects of Language.* New York: Harcourt, Brace & World, 1968.

Clark, H. H., and Clark, E. V. *Psychology and Language.* New York: Harcourt Brace Jovanovich, 1977.

Dahl, O., *et al. Logic in Linguistics.* New York: Cambridge University Press, 1977.

Dinneen, F. P. *An Introduction to General Linguistics.* New York: Holt, Rinehart & Winston, 1967. (Includes excerpts from the writings of Boas, Sapir, Bloomfield, and Chomsky, with exposition.)

Dubois-Charlier, F., and Galmiche, M. *La Sémantique générative.* Paris: Didier-Larousse, 1972.

Fillmore, C. J. "The Case for Case," in E. Bach and R. T. Harms, *Universals in Linguistic Theory.* New York: Holt, Rinehart & Winston, 1968.

Fodor, J. A., and Katz, J. J. *The Structure of Language: Readings in the Philosophy of Language.* Englewood Cliffs, N.J.: Prentice-Hall, 1964.

Fodor, J. A. *et al. The Psychology of Language.* New York: McGraw-Hill, 1974.

Fodor, J. A. *Semantics: Theories of Meaning in Generative Linguistics.* New York: Crowell, 1977.

Greene, J. *Psycholinguistics: Chomsky and Psychology.* Baltimore: Penguin, 1972.

Harman, G. *On Noam Chomsky: Selected Essays.* New York: Doubleday, 1974.

Huddleston, R. D. *Introduction to English Transformational Syntax.* London: Longmans, 1976.

Hymes, D. Review of first edition of Lyons, *Noam Chomsky,* in *Language* 48 (1972): 416–27. Reprinted in G. Harman, *On Noam Chomsky.*

Hymes, D. *Foundations in Sociolinguistics.* Philadelphia: University of Pennsylvania Press, 1974.

Lees, R. B. Review of Chomsky, *Syntactic Structures,* in *Language* 33 (1957): 375–407. Reprinted in G. Harman, *On Noam Chomsky.*

Lyons, J. *Introduction to Theoretical Linguistics.* New York: Cambridge University Press, 1968.

Lyons, J. (ed.) *New Horizons in Linguistics.* London: Penguin, 1970.

Marshall, J. C. Review of Esper, *Mentalism and Objectivism in Linguistics*, in *Semiotica* 2 (1970): 227–293.

Matthews, P. H. Review of Chomsky, *Aspects of the Theory of Syntax*, in *Journal of Linguistics* 3 (1967): 119–52.

Oldfield, R. C., and Marshall, J. C. (eds.) *Language.* London: Penguin, 1968.

Partee, B. H. "Montague Grammar and Transformational Grammar," in *Linguistic Inquiry* 6 (1975): 203–300.

Peters, S., and Ritchie, R. "Non-filtering and Local Filtering Transformational Grammar," in K. J. J. Hintikka *et al.*, *Approaches to Natural Language.* Dordrecht, Netherlands: Reidel, 1973.

Robins, R. H. *A Short History of Linguistics.* London: Longmans, 1967.

Sampson, G. *The Form of Language.* London: Weidenfeld & Nicolson, 1975.

Sapir, E. *Language.* New York: Harcourt, Brace & World, 1921.

Sevren, P. A. M. *Semantic Syntax.* London: Oxford University Press, 1974.

Slobin, D. I. *Psycholinguistics.* Glenview, Ill.: Scott, Foresman, 1971.

Steinberg, D. D., and Jakobovits, L. (eds.) *Semantics: An Interdisciplinary Reader in Philosophy, Linguistics and Psychology.* New York: Cambridge University Press, 1971.

Those who are interested in the wider philosophical and psychological implications of Chomsky's work might well begin with the enlarged edition of *Language and Mind* (1972), going on from that to *Reflections on Language* (1976), which is very largely a restatement of his position on some of the more controversial issues. *Problems of Freedom and Knowledge* (1971) gives what is probably the clearest and most readable account by Chomsky himself of what he sees as a synthesis of his linguistic, philosophical, and political thought—a synthesis determined, at all points, by his acceptance of what, following Bertrand Russell, he refers to as "the humanistic conception of man."

As far as Chomsky's work in linguistics is concerned: *Syntactic Structures* (1957), interpreted perhaps in the light of the review by Lees and the Introduction to Chomsky's *The Logical Structure of Linguistic Theory* (1975), is still, in my view, the best starting point. *Topics in the Theory of Generative Grammar* (1966) gives a clearer account of the so-called standard theory than *Aspects of the Theory of Syntax* (1965) does. (Excerpts from *Syntactic Structures*, *Topics in the Theory of Generative Grammar*, *Aspects of the Theory of Syntax*, and other works are conveniently brought together, with a linking editorial commentary, in Allen and Van Buren's *Chomsky: Selected Readings*.) There is no comparable account of Chomsky's more recent extended standard theory: *Studies on Semantics in Generative Grammar* (1972) contains the major transitional articles. Of Chomsky's more technical writings, "On the Notion 'Rule of Grammar'" (1961) is recommended. "Introduction to the Formal Analysis of Natural Languages" (1963) and "Formal Properties of Grammars" (1963) give a much fuller (and more technical) account of the subject than I do in Appendix 1, and either these two articles or the more recently published *The Logical Structure of Linguistic Theory* (1975) should be read by anyone who wishes to go farther into the formalism.

The works by authors other than Chomsky listed above were chosen for their relevance to the topics dealt with in this volume and, with one or two exceptions, for their accessibility. Three rather different, but equally reliable, introductions to transformational grammar are listed: Huddleston's is perhaps the most readable and Akmajian and Heny's the most comprehensive; Bach is especially good on the formalism and the implications of the more recent developments. The book by Dahl *et al.* is written specifically for linguists or prospective linguists; unlike most introductions to logic it has something to say about modern formal semantics and intensional logic (not to mention categorial grammar). A clear and readable account of the work done so far in semantics within the framework of Chomskyan and, to a certain extent, post-Chomskyan generative grammar is to be found in Janet Fodor's book.

The Fodor and Katz and the Steinberg and Jakobovits collections contain important articles from the earlier and later periods of generative grammar, respectively. They are both intended to bring out the philosophical and psychological implications of Chomskyan linguistics. Harman's volume is more specifically philosophical in orientation. Oldfield and Marshall's, on the other hand, is psychological. The Lyons collection, *New Horizons in Linguistics*, is now a little dated, but it has a good Bibliography and, unlike the other anthologies listed here, is made up wholly of articles written for nonspecialists.

Each of the five listed works on psycholinguistics has something different to recommend it. Judith Greene's is the one that is most directly related to the subject of this book: It gives a good account of Chomskyan generative grammar (with a brief indication of some of the emergent post-Chomskyan trends) and of the psycholinguistic work that it had inspired up to about 1970. Jean Aitchison's is more general in its coverage: Intended for nonspecialists, it is lively in style and up-to-date; it includes a summary of the biological and ethological evidence for the "nativist" hypothesis, and an account of the recent experiments with chimpanzees. Slobin's book is also designed for nonspecialists: It overlaps with both Judith Greene's and Jean Aitchison's but also deals with semantics and the relationship between language and cognition. The book by Clark and Clark is similar in coverage to Slobin's but different in emphasis and more up-to-date. Rather more demanding is *The Psychology of Language*, by Fodor *et al.*; unless one already has some background in psychology, it is probably better to read one of the other works first.

Geoffrey Sampson's book discusses Chomsky from a point of view that differs, in certain respects, from the point of view adopted here. It is forthright in tone and, at times, deliberately controversial, especially on the philosophical issues; but it is very readable and contains a valuable Bibliography.

On some of the more recent Chomskyan and post-Chomskyan work referred to in Chapter ix, it is difficult to find anything of a nontechnical nature. Much of what I have mentioned has not so far found its way into the textbooks and more popular treatments of linguistics. The beginnings of post-*Aspects* transformational grammar are very briefly described in my article in the *New Horizons* volume; and many of the more general books listed above, published since 1970, say something about case grammar (though usually only Fillmore's version of it) and generative semantics. The reader's attention is drawn, in addition, to the books by Sevren and (in French) by Dubois-Charlier and Galmiche; both of these are concerned exclusively with generative semantics. For the rest, I must advise the reader to consult recent issues of such journals as *Foundations of Language, Journal of Linguistics, Language, Lingua, Linguistic Inquiry, Linguistics and Philosophy,* and *Theoretical Linguistics.*

INDEX

A selection of books published by Penguin is listed on the following pages. For a complete list of books available from Penguin in the United States, write to Dept. DG, Penguin Books, 299 Murray Hill Parkway, East Rutherford, New Jersey 07073.

PSYCHOLINGUISTICS: CHOMSKY AND PSYCHOLOGY

Judith Greene

How is man able to produce a virtually unlimited number of possible sentences? Chomsky's theory of grammar that forced this question on the consciousness of psychologists has led to a revolution in the study of language. In explaining that revolution Dr. Greene takes the reader into a deep analysis of both the linguistic and the psychological aspects of the new science of psycholinguistics.

SOCIOLINGUISTICS: AN INTRODUCTION

Peter Trudgill

The Eskimo language has several words for snow; female speakers of Mongolian may have different vowels from men; a German living near the Dutch frontier may understand a visitor from Amsterdam more readily than one from Munich. Such items are the raw material of sociolinguistics, the branch of linguistics which studies the links between language and society. In this introductory survey Peter Trudgill shows how class, race, sex, religion, environment, and region are among the factors that father differences in and between languages; and how, on the other hand, language may sometimes condition thought, and so, indirectly, society.

LANGUAGE AND SOCIAL CONTEXT

Edited by Pier Paolo Giglioli

Even the simplest of spoken statements may provide far more information about the speaker—his social standing, his immediate situation, his relationship with his audience—than he might ever suspect. Sociolinguistics focuses on all the varied aspects of the social organization of speech. We share a linguistic repertoire with members of our social networks (and failure to "fit in" linguistically may have far-reaching consequences); we also alter our speech patterns according to the specific social situation.

Some other titles in
PENGUIN MODERN MASTERS

This acclaimed series presents studies of men who
have changed and will change the thought of our
time. Although the work of these leading figures is
difficult and often misunderstood, the volumes in Penguin Modern Masters succeed in delineating and clari-
fying it. As the series' editor, Frank Kermode, has
said, "The authors of these volumes are themselves
masters, and they have written their books in the
belief that general discussion of their subjects will
henceforth be more informed and more exciting than
ever before."

ANTONIN ARTAUD
Martin Esslin

CLAUDE LEVI-STRAUSS
Edmund Leach

EINSTEIN
Jeremy Bernstein

KARL MARX
David McLellan

T. S. ELIOT
Stephen Spender

FERDINAND DE SAUSSURE
Jonathan Culler

FRIEDRICH ENGELS
David McLellan

JOHN MAYNARD KEYNES
D. E. Moggridge